THE
ROGER
CARAS
PET
BOOK

THE ROGER CARAS PET BOOK

Roger A. Caras

Holt, Rinehart and Winston   New York

Library of Congress Cataloging in Publication Data
Caras, Roger A
    The Roger Caras pet book.

    1. Pets.   2. Dogs.   I. Title.
SF413.C37   636.08'87   76–4730
ISBN 0–03–017506–2

Printed in the United States of America
10 9 8 7 6 5 4 3 2 1

This book is for Guy Coheleach, Jr. His allotment was ten years and he never had time to become hard or cynical about his fellow man. For the full measure of his life he knew only love. It surrounded him, it was everywhere he went, it came from within and without. As a child he was what all of us would like to mature to be—wise and at peace with his world.

CONTENTS

5 OTHER PETS

INTRODUCTION

On November 22, 1969, the first edition of "Pets and Wildlife" was broadcast over the CBS Radio Network. Except for eighty-five dollars I had once received for appearing on Arthur Godfrey's radio show, that program gave me the first money I had ever earned in broadcasting.

It was an experiment, really. CBS wanted to see if there was interest in a pet show, although they did not think of it as something that could last for very long. They were so uncertain that they signed me to a thirteen-week contract calling for two shows a week. They told me they were not at all convinced that there were twenty-six good shows in the idea, but it is to their credit that they were willing to give it a chance.

The original "Pets and Wildlife" stayed on CBS for just over seven hundred shows, somewhat beyond the original uncertain projection of twenty-six. Then, for programming reasons and because the whole picture of network and affiliate relationships was changing, the show went off the air. Within hours the NBC radio network had picked it up, and for a year it was a part of "Monitor" as "Report from the World of Animals." Then "Monitor" came apart and "Report" went off. Very shortly CBS invited me to come back, and "Pets and Wildlife" has, at the time of this writing, been on the air almost eleven hundred times. It is heard now as part of a daily electronic "feed" to the CBS Radio Stations News Service. Recorded in New York, it is fed out through Washington, D.C., to the seven major radio markets.

Doing "Pets and Wildlife" in its various incarnations over the years has been a great deal of fun. It has given me an opportunity to meet a lot of people and assemble a lot of information. It has also brought in thousands of letters and made a lot of friends. It is meant as a one-to-one broadcast, one person talking to another about something of mutual interest and concern. It is a show that has gotten through to a lot of listeners, judging from their letters.

Some of the letters are inadvertently funny. One woman wrote to tell me she was certain her veterinarian was cheating her. She said he was insisting on giving her dog distemper shots although he knew full well that her dog had a very nice disposition.

Some letters are sad—very often they are that. Children write to speak of pets recently departed, and old people are often lonely because a pet has gone. One young couple wrote and asked me to referee their divorce since a dog was involved in the property settlement, and they were having a terrible battle over who got him.

People also get into terrible battles over such questions as which snake is the worst in the whole world, or whether Peter Benchley was telling the truth in *Jaws,* and they write in to have the argument settled. We try to play King Solomon in those cases, for two listeners are involved.

There is some hate mail, of course, but it is almost always unsigned. In one letter that was signed, a gentleman whom I assume disagreed with something I had said started out by calling me a "child-molesting, impotent, homosexual communist out for a quick buck." After that he got mean. My wife and kids were delighted and wanted to frame it. I resisted.

Most of the letters we get at CBS, however, ask basic questions such as which dog is right for a given family. That can't be answered, of course; all we can do is profile each breed over a period of time so people can make their own decisions. In the third section of this book, we have included programs on the fifty most popular breeds as listed for 1975 by the American Kennel Club, plus a few others in certain groups.

The scripts for this book, and these are all scripts, were selected from over a thousand used on CBS and a year's worth from NBC—that is, all those dealing with pets and matters of pet ownership. Generally, they represent information most often requested by listeners, or are those broadcasts most frequently requested in the form of transcripts by people who heard them in a car somewhere and wanted to have them to review at leisure.

We have included some scripts on horses, although horses are actually not pets. But as so many people, including my wife and daughter, do think of them as pets, we felt some representation was warranted.

You will notice that in the sections on dogs and cats there are no reports on breeding. That is because I do not believe pets should be bred. There are already far too many dogs and cats in this world, and pet owners should not add to that misery. Owners of superb examples of purebred animals who feel they can make a serious contribution to the breed by passing that animal's genetic potential along should consult a veterinarian before they start breeding their animal. No one else should consider doing it.

Don Hutter, my editor at Holt, Rinehart and Winston, whose idea it was to turn these scripts into a book, worked long and hard at selection. Because the eye reading from the page makes demands different from those of the ear listening to the radio, stylistic changes were needed throughout, but the content remains unchanged. Where Don felt there were holes that needed filling if a mountain of scripts was to become a book, we conferred, and when we agreed (which was often, because Don is very persuasive), I ran off, wrote the script, broadcast it over CBS, and delivered it to Don. One way or another, the mountain of scripts got culled, rearranged, combined, edited, and augmented, and this book is the result.

One last thing, a personal enthusiasm: If you really care about the subject matter of this book, if it interests and concerns you, think about what you can do to make life easier for animals. You might want to join The Humane Society of the United States. They are at 2100 L Street NW, Washington, D.C. 20037. Tell them Caras over at CBS sent you.

East Hampton, N.Y.

PETS AND PET OWNERSHIP

The Psychology of Pet Ownership: A surprising amount of time is spent trying to explain why people like having pets around. A number of books have been written on the subject, some of them on an academic level. New studies are being published all the time.

People apparently have had pets around for somewhere between twenty-five and fifty thousand years. There must be something to it. Pets fill a need, that is a good starting point. People like having them around. They may be kept for their great physical beauty, like a Siamese cat, an Afghan Hound, or a Borzoi, or because they are friends, like a Boston Terrier or again a Siamese cat. They may be family, like Toy Poodles and little Schnauzers, or grown-up pals and work companions like the Retrievers and other field dogs. Basically, they serve a need. They provide something that the people who have them want to add to their lives. Some critics, and why there should be critics of pet ownership I can't imagine, say that pets replace people in some people's lives. They say that as if they have discovered gold. Of course pets often replace people, but when people are gone—dead or away or whatever fate has decreed—what is wrong with replacing their human love with animal love? It is better than a high bridge and a deep river. If people need pets because they are lonely, why is that to be criticized or even discussed? It is their private business.

I think it is equally silly to criticize people who neither need nor want pets. That, too, is their business. Those of us who find pleasure in animals may think these others are missing something, but it may be, probably is, what they want to miss. I am sure I am missing something because I don't really appreciate chamber music, but that is my way. What it comes down to, I guess, is everybody minding his own business and letting other people do what they want to do, what they feel is right and good and fulfilling for them. As the kids say, you do your own thing.

Responsible Pet Ownership: There is growing concern in both urban and suburban environments about the way people allow their pets to annoy and even endanger their neighbors. I have owned cats and dogs all of my life, but if I had my way, I would deprive anyone of the right to own a pet who did not properly care for that pet or did not properly regard the rights of his neighbors. Owning a pet, like owning a car, a plane, or a boat, carries with it responsibilities. The fact that an animal can suffer while a machine cannot is yet another consideration.

No pet owner should allow his dog to soil playground or park areas where children play. Footpaths and crosswalks and certainly sidewalks should be kept clean. In the city and suburbs, pets should be walked on leashes or should be kept on the owner's property and not allowed to wander, for their own sakes as well as those of their human neighbors. Any dog that shows signs of being a biter should be disposed of or so restrained and contained that it cannot be a danger to other people and their pets. Neither the paper boy nor the mailman should have to fear for his life; cartoons to the contrary notwithstanding, there is nothing funny about a biting dog. Fifty million dollars has been suggested as the actual amount of the annual medical bill for repairing victims of dog bite. Excessive barkers that disturb the neighborhood should be trained to desist, and if the owner can't manage the problem himself there are schools that can. In fact, professional obedience training is a very good idea for most dog owners. All dogs should be inoculated against disease, not only for their own sakes, but so they cannot spread disease to other animals. All pets should be properly and humanely maintained, and if a pet can no longer be so kept, it is unthinkable that it be set loose to fend for itself. Unthinkable, yet millions of people do just that every year.

A lot of people are reevaluating the role of the pet in human society. It will be too bad if the crimes of the few curtail the rights of the many. Pet owning is immensely satisfying and a very important element in the emotional well-being of many people. It is also a task, a responsibility, and a clear call to be good neighbors and considerate human beings.

The Right to Own a Pet: Does a person, any person, have the right to own a pet? It is an issue that has come before the lower courts and bureaucratic referees many times in recent years, and the answer still has not been resolved. Does a city housing development have the right to pass a rule that no pets are allowed? I think it is clearly a matter of civil rights. A small, fatherless youngster being raised in a city housing project by a mother who is on welfare has no options about how and where he or she will live. That is clear enough. Then, without reason, insofar as this youngster is concerned, some bureaucrat says "no pets." The kid's pet hasn't created a nuisance because the kid's pet doesn't exist. The ruling, then, is arbitrary. Over on another street lives a family in a co-op that costs fifteen hundred dollars a month and has porters and doormen falling over each other for tips. No one, but no one, is telling these people that they can't have their Poodle or Pekingese. Is that not discrimination, and are not civil rights being violated? It does seem that a judge in a court high enough to set precedent had better address him- or herself to this problem and resolve it.

I believe it is arbitrary and an unconstitutional intrusion on privacy to say that a citizen may not exercise the right of ownership in or on property he or she leases, or that is leased in his or her name, simply on the suspicion that the exercise of that right may one day prove a nuisance. We do not tell apartment dwellers that they may not own TV and stereo and radio sets because they might play them too loudly. Yet, I would venture the guess that more people make pests of themselves with their stereo sets than with barking dogs.

We have questions here, not answers, because the answers are in the realm of constitutional law. What is needed is precedent, a clear statement of what the rights of people are when it comes to owning a pet —not the right to abuse their neighbors with one, just the right to own one.

The Role of the Pet: I once got a very angry letter from a woman who did not want her children to have a pet and who felt that I was coming on "too strong" on behalf of pet ownership. She felt that I was making it seem as if anyone who felt as she did about animals was a bad parent.

Of course there are many reasons why some people should not have a pet. They may have allergies, there may be incompatibility with certain members of the family, there may be phobias, a family may travel a great deal. There are clauses in leases, there can be financial considerations . . . lots of reasons, including the fact that some people don't like animals well enough to keep them around. All this is legitimate. If you can't have pets or don't want pets, so be it. But what are the values of pet ownership in a home with children? My answers do not imply that these values are available only from pets, but I know from long experience that pets do help children grow up. In a home with pets, children can learn to be gentle. They can learn to care for creatures more helpless than themselves. They can learn responsibility, the life-and-death meaning of responsibility, for their pets will die without their attention. There are all kinds of love in this world: some you learn from parents, some from siblings, some from grandparents, some from teddy bears, some from friends, and some from pets. And you do learn some things from a pet that no human can teach you. It is up to the individual parent to decide whether or not that is important.

There are lots of ways of instilling a reverence for life in children. Pet ownership is one way. There are many ways of teaching children that pain is a universal experience; pet ownership is a way. Children should be given some contact with the natural world no matter where they live. Starting when they are very young, they need a bridge into another kind of world to help them expand and grow (note how often animals figure in children's literature). One way to build that bridge is with a pet. There are other ways, but that is one. You don't have to have animals in your life to be happy, but I find that they help much more than many nonowners realize.

Pets and Child Development: Since caveman days, our human species has somehow known that kids and animals belong together. We in contemporary America have built a multibillion-dollar industry based on the fact that kids often find it easier growing up with a pet by their side.

Psychiatrists and therapists are using pets now; one New York doctor, Boris Levinson, refers to dogs as canine co-therapists. A school for kids in trouble, north of New York City, has dogs for the youngsters to relate to. When the pressure builds on a young person, when there doesn't seem any way to bridge his or her own inner turmoil to the outside world, a pet can help. A pet doesn't say "don't play with matches." A pet doesn't scold you for a fifty-five score in a Spanish test. A pet doesn't care if you keep your room neat or do your homework or wash your hands or get a haircut. A pet is there with love, no questions asked, no matter what. When everyone around you is concerned about your future, including what you are doing to it by saying "ain't" or not brushing your teeth, a pet is as existentialist as you want to be. It is here today, living and loving today. But there is something bigger and even more important than that. A pet requires care. Without lecturing, it somehow makes you want to accept responsibility. It hurts you to see your pet ill cared for, hungry or thirsty, so you chip in and do what you must for your friend, and it isn't because you are afraid of the consequences if you don't. And then there are the times of loneliness and perhaps a little alienation (that come to everyone), and the sense of touch helps. You are not alone when your fingertips bring you a message of pleasure. That is why we stroke our pets; it is touch, contact, a sense of bridging out of ourselves into the world beyond. The ways in which a pet can help a child develop are many and not all cataloged yet, much less understood.

Pets as Gifts: A living, loving addition to the family is an appropriate gift, especially for Christmas, but the gift must be matched to the person. It is not at all amusing to find yourself with an animal you do not care about. Then the animal suffers. Cage birds are lovely for elderly people and for kids with allergies that rule out cats and dogs. An aquarium is perfect for the scientifically minded youngster and the gadgeteer; often a great idea for a husband, to add color and movement to his shop, his study, or his office. A terrarium also makes a fine gift, particularly for a youngster interested in science or in nature studies. There are small reptiles, amphibians, and mammals that will do well on a bookshelf in a child's bedroom.

How about exotic pets? They are generally a poor idea. Monkeys, ocelots, most wild creatures make unsatisfactory pets. You waste your money when you buy them while encouraging a traffic in cruelty, for these animals do suffer in captivity.

Generally speaking, the best pets and the best gifts are puppies and kittens. While it is a fine idea to buy your cage birds, your terrarium and aquarium animals from pet shops, that is not where you buy your dog. If you want a purebred dog, see a professional breeder who has devoted his life to one breed. Pet shops buy from amateur or accidental neighborhood breeders or from puppy factories, where there is little attention to breed standards. One such puppy mill offers sixty-four breeds of dogs. How can a breeder devote his life to perfecting sixty-four breeds? If you want something less expensive than a purebred animal, there are literally millions of mixed-breed puppies and kittens in need of homes. For a few dollars (or nothing!) you can adopt a puppy or kitten from a shelter. Whatever you do decide to get, puppy or kitten, aquarium, gerbils, white mice, a harmless snake, or a bird, match the animal to the needs, the spirit, and the capabilities of the recipient. Don't give him more animal than he can handle or really wants, or you are being cruel to the animal.

Cats and Dogs Together: We live in an era when the ownership of two cats, not one, is the status symbol. It is also a time when many families have more than one pet. A common question is whether or not cats and dogs can successfully share a home. A surprising number of people believe that the mixture is impossible. Categorically, that is nonsense.

While there *are* dog-hating cats and cat-baiting dogs that are beyond conversion, they are more the exception than the rule. Paradoxically, a cat that has established itself in a home will generally accept a dog into the family more readily than it will accept another cat. Cats and dogs will almost always get along splendidly if human beings don't try to engineer the relationship.

Dogs and cats have distinctly different personalities, it is true, but they also have a great many traits in common. They each like their creature comforts and, if living together, will have to sort out the details between them, such as who gets which spot in the sun at what time of the day. Very often, cats and dogs that live together take the easy way out; they call for "no contest" and share the good places curled up together.

The *best* way to establish this mixed pet bag, of course, is to get two young animals and start them off together. It should take the average puppy-kitten combination about thirty minutes to become friends for life. However, if your family already includes either a mature cat or a grown dog, there is no reason not to introduce the other, preferably as a young animal. The introduction of a cat and a dog (or a cat and a cat for that matter) is bound to be accompanied, on the part of the cat, by ceremonial hissing and spitting. The dog is more likely to want to sniff and get acquainted. He may even want to try out an experimental chase and tussle. The cat will soon put him right on that issue.

What the owner of newly acquainted animals must realize is that nature will sort things out. Let the animals alone. They'll test each other, they'll skulk around furniture, and you may hear an occasional explosive hiss or two when the strangers meet at the intersection of hall and kitchen door, but those are the games animals play. The cat may even want to spend a day or two sulking under a bed, but that will pass. The happy combination of dog and cat has worked itself out millions of times and will in your home as well. The animals are better equipped to solve their own social problems than you are.

Pet Population: It is estimated that there are between 42 and 47 million family-owned dogs in the United States today. Which means that over fifty percent of American families have dogs as pets. The same pet industry survey puts family-owned cats at about 30 million. Unfortunately, this still leaves millions of strays and unwanted puppies and kittens, born at the rate of thousands an hour, night and day. It takes well over $100 million a year just to destroy these poor, bedeviled creatures.

Twenty-three percent of the farms in the United States have both cats and dogs in residence, an incidence much higher than the national average; only about four percent of big-city residences have both kinds of pets at the same time. But, interesting enough, the percentage of farms having dogs is not really that much higher than the percentage of city apartments. If that seems strange, keep in mind that dogs are called upon for work very rarely these days, even on farms. The farmer usually keeps dogs around for the same reason the urbanite does, because he loves them.

Since the end of World War II, there has been a great deal of interest in dog shows, and somewhere between twenty-five and thirty percent of the pet dogs in America are purebred. Dog shows in America today number more than twenty-five hundred a year, cat shows around two hundred.

In case you think you know America's dog tastes, what are the five top breeds in American Kennel Club registration? If you thought Poodle, German Shepherd, Irish Setter, Doberman Pinscher, and Beagle, you were right. The second five are Dachshund, Cocker Spaniel, Miniature Schnauzer, Labrador Retriever, and Collie. The second ten may contain a few surprises for you: Shetland Sheepdog, Golden Retriever, St. Bernard, Pekingese, Siberian Husky, Great Dane, Brittany Spaniel, Yorkshire Terrier, Lhasa Apso, and Chihuahua. Would your list have looked anything like this? If I had been guessing and not referring, I would have put the Boxer and Boston Terrier up there, and never dreamed of including the Chihuahua or the Brittany Spaniel. But those are the facts.

According to the Pet Food Institute, Americans spend over $2.25 billion a year on prepared pet foods. There are fifteen thousand different foods on the market today just for dogs and cats. The first commercially prepared dog biscuit was marketed in England in 1855. It wasn't until the 1930s that canned cat food appeared. The industry has come a long way since then. The average supermarket today earns almost two percent of its total revenue from pet foods. What all of these facts add up to is that we need our pets as much as they need us.

Your Veterinarian: The first veterinarian to graduate from an institution of higher learning received his diploma from Cornell University in 1876. The science of the D.V.M. has been expanding ever since. For the pet owner, the veterinarian is a vitally important person, the key to a healthy, fulfilling pet. There is no alternative to knowing and utilizing the services of a skilled practitioner.

The question often arises, what should the pet owner look for in a veterinarian? How does one tell if a vet is good or bad? Both kinds are around. The key, I think, is communication. You must be able to communicate with the person to whom you are entrusting your animal friend's life. You don't use a physician, dentist, or lawyer with whom you feel ill at ease, perhaps even alienated, and the same yardstick should apply when you select a veterinarian.

No veterinarian should object to showing you around his hospital. Your nose will tell you quickly enough what kind of an institution he runs. Obviously, a dirty, smelly cage area or a treatment room that is unkempt is an early warning sign. I watch to see if the veterinarian wipes the examining table down with a disinfectant before putting an animal on it. Are his hands and clothes reasonably clean? The hands of a veterinarian are hard used in the course of the day and are often discolored by the materials he works with. Still, there is a look about a person, and no veterinarian I would want to associate with works in filth or fails to provide protection for incoming animals against the diseases of the outgoing ones.

It may be true that a veterinarian can be extremely skillful without being an animal lover, but I feel better when I know my animal's doctor likes animals. Watch for the way the man or woman handles your pet, how much reassuring is done, how roughly the animal is handled. Simple observation can tell you a great deal.

A veterinarian who cannot be reached off-hours or who does not have an arrangement for handling night-time and weekend emergencies is not for me. I look for that. I don't think a veterinarian should be called out on Christmas Eve because your dog has an itch, but emergencies can and do arise. They do not always conform to office hours.

There are few mysteries in the veterinarian-client relationship. Look and ask questions, and you will soon find out what you have to know in order to make intelligent decisions and to be reassured that your pet is in good hands.

Animal Shelters: Whatever you call it—a pound, a shelter, a humane society, a rescue league—the organization, civil or private, in your community that is responsible for collecting stray, injured, and unwanted animals faces an almost impossible task. Your support and understanding are desperately needed. The number of animals without homes is tragic. Unwanted puppies and kittens are born every day of the year by the tens of thousands. We spend over $100 million every year collecting them and destroying them. It isn't a nice job, in fact it is backbreaking and heart-breaking; still, it has to be done. How well it is done, how humanely the animals are collected, maintained, and placed for adoption or destroyed, depends on support within the community. An indifferent community is going to do an indifferent job. Just what does indifference mean? It means pain. It means millions of little tragedies every year. It means overworked, underpaid people who will destroy a stray dog without bothering to register it, cage it, feed it, and give it water. In most communities, they are supposed to keep it five to ten days. In others, where a pet may be disposed of merely because it shows up at the end of a working day, parents with frantic children can appear the next morning, looking for their pet, but by then it is too late. Does this happen often? Thousands of times a year. There are shelters where the help cannot possibly use humane methods to destroy unwanted dogs and cats because they pile up in crates faster than they can be killed off, hundreds every day. We may never see these things happen, we may never even hear about them, but they happen and they are our fault. We are careless and put off having our animals spayed and neutered, or we never have it done at all. Result? Too many animals for the homes available, by the ratio of scores to one. Then we turn away and fail to make the local humane society or shelter our business. Result? Stark horror. It is not a pretty story, but the truth doesn't have to be pretty. Resolve to help, resolve to care, accept your obligations as a human being. Check into and join your local humane society. Pitch in and help their adoption and educational programs.

The Humane Movement: There are a good many humane societies in the United States. Some are local, like the excellent Massachusetts Society for the Prevention of Cruelty to Animals (which runs one of the world's finest veterinary hospitals, Angell Memorial in Boston), and some are national, like The Humane Society of the United States in Washington, D.C., a national educational organization that fights for reform. HSUS keeps full-time investigators on the road, specialists in zoo and wildlife institutions, predator control experts, and others as well. Once upon a time, people who cared what happened when horses were beaten to their knees on public streets were considered odd. People who stopped other people from burning dogs and cats to death for laughs, well, they were strange. They were the kind of people who read books like *Black Beauty* and wept.

Things have changed, and now people who demand that the rights of animals be recognized are no longer so much in the minority or so easily put off. They have prevailed in courts of law again and again. America is a nation of animal lovers. Millions of us have dogs and cats, birds and fish, and over 180 million people are logged into our national parks each year. There is no way of knowing how many visit state parks and national and local wildlife refuges. More people visit our zoos than attend all spectator sporting events combined. The Milwaukee Zoo alone, for example, has 1.6 million visitors a year; and we have over 250 zoos.

So, we are a nation of animal lovers. But we have not always recognized the suffering some of us have heaped on animals. There are still barbarisms like leghold traps, predator control with poisoning campaigns, incredible abuses in uncontrolled slaughterhouses—a long list. But all of these hangovers from the dark ages are now being zeroed in on by our humane societies, and their days are numbered. There is nothing wrong with being gentle. It is not even a crime to be sentimental. People who are humane are better, not worse, than their fellow men. I think we should recognize that fact.

Abandoned Cats and Dogs: Every June, millions of urban Americans migrate to lakefront, beach, farm, and mountains. Tens of thousands of these vacationers stop by pounds and shelters and adopt a puppy or a kitten for a summer's fun. Some of these people know full well they will never keep these pets. They are summer animals only. In the fall, they are abandoned by the thousands. In every resort community in America, the feral dog and cat population soars in the fall. Then it declines as the animals are killed by cars, shot by farmers, and die of starvation, disease, and trauma. What do people tell their kids who watch them treat a trusting, living creature like an old shoe? What lessons do kids learn from such people? More wondrous yet, what do such people tell themselves when they lie down in the dark at night? How little they must think of themselves!

The people who do this kind of thing can be black or white or of Asian origin; they wear white collars or blue collars; their cars can be Fords or Rolls-Royces. They come from all segments of our vast and varied population, but they have this in common: they are the worst people in the world. I hope this is read by someone who has done this kind of thing, or is thinking of it, for such irresponsible people need and deserve to see and hear their crimes discussed. It is the most arrant nonsense to think or state that abandoned pets can care for themselves. The few that can often have to resort to killing wildlife or livestock, and that is no help to farms or those who manage our wilderness areas. There is no legitimate role for these animals in the disrupted ecosystem we have created around us. Abandoning animals is criminal. The fact that our laws do not always say so is yet another criminal aspect of life in America today. If you know of someone who has abandoned an animal, how about making him known to his neighbors and to the police? Be a friend of the court and a friend of the animals. Make these criminals pay just as much as the law prescribes.

Petnapping: It would almost seem like a joke if there weren't tragic truth in this decidedly unpleasant business of petnapping. No, it is no joke, though it is a very profitable racket in many parts of the country. The perpetrators drive through neighborhood after neighborhood looking for unguarded dogs, especially those that are allowed to wander. An offer of a dog biscuit or other bait and the truck door slams. Miserable parents and heartbroken kids scour the area until long after dark; then come the phone calls and the visits to the pound, the police, the veterinarian, with no chance for success.

Where do the dogs go? The young purebreds go to breeding farms, very often, and are used to supply some pet shops with offspring; the papers issued in these cases are phony, of course. Stolen breeding stock is kept in tiny cages. Some animals are sold to laboratories—the mongrels usually, and some purebreds, particularly females that have been spayed. Good hunting dogs—Setters, Retrievers, Spaniels, Hounds, and Pointers—are sold to hunters.

There are wholesale dog markets. One in Mississippi comes to mind, where truckloads of dogs are bought and sold in a single day. Humane investigators covering this market report endless violations, but so far, the authorities refuse to prosecute. They turn their heads and shrug at the atrocities: dogs are tied on leads so short they can't sit or lie down, or they are tied to fences and bumpers and left in the sun without water. It is mass cruelty, but the government of Mississippi

just won't see it that way. There are other wholesale
markets as well, and the men and sometimes the women
who deal in some of them are like characters out of
Dickens. I guess you could call them the bottom rung.
How do you keep your dog out of their hands? Simple.
You keep your dog at home where it can't be stolen,
and you let it exercise under your supervision. If dogs
start disappearing in your neighborhood, you had better wonder if the petnappers aren't working your part
of the state. They love the suburbs, since the space between residences favors their actions, but they do hit
farm country and cities as well. Let the punishment
fit the crime, they say. . . . Well, I hate to tell you what
the punishment should be for this crime, in my estima-
tion. After all, I am supposed to be civilized.

The Battered-Pet Syndrome: We have all heard about
the battered-child syndrome, that absolute horror
which I, for one, really don't understand. Having raised
two youngsters myself, I cannot conceive of putting out
a cigarette in the middle of a child's back, no matter
what he or she has done. Well, now we have a new horror. Humane groups are reporting an increased occurrence of battered pets. I certainly don't put this
matter on a par with battered children, but it is something we should be aware of and think about. From
what I have been able to learn, people hard hit by an
adverse personal situation sometimes take out their
hostility and frustration on cats and dogs, their own or
those belonging to other people. Now, I have known
bad times the way everyone probably has at some point
in his or her life. I have known anger and even rage. But
I will be confounded if I can understand beating a
living thing, whether a child or an animal, to let off
steam. I don't care how many jobs a guy hasn't been

able to get or how mad he is over politics or delays in tax refunds—inflicting pain, even agony and death, on living creatures unable to defend themselves is sick. Help is obviously needed, and I mean psychiatric help. I don't imagine that anyone reading this is an animal beater (or a child beater), but you may know one; it may be a neighbor, or even a close acquaintance. You have an obligation if you do know of such a person. You should call either the police or a local humane group and ask for action. That is a clear obligation on the part of a civilized man or women. Almost as baffling as the child beaters are the neighbors who tolerate it, and the same goes, on a different plane, obviously, with animal torture. If someone you know is so unstable that he can only retain his sanity by torture, you are as guilty as he is if you do not intervene. Perhaps you are more guilty since your excuse isn't mental illness, but simply a wish not to get involved. Think about that, unpleasant though it may be.

Euthanasia: There are times when we, as responsible adult citizens, must consider or discuss extremely painful subjects, no matter how difficult it may be—subjects like pet euthanasia, the mercy killing of our animal friends.

One should know, for instance, how animal euthanasia is done. In some places it is done humanely, and in others, in ways almost too brutal to contemplate. The most humane method of all is the merciful needle with an overdose of barbiturates. But, it is also one of the relatively more expensive methods and the drug laws can still make it illegal for nondoctors—in this case, nonveterinarians—to possess the necessary drugs, needles, and syringes. In many areas, it is the humane-shelter technicians who do what must be done, for there simply are not enough veterinarians in this country to perform the euthanasia that is required. If you are a person concerned with animal welfare, then it is your responsibility to know how it is being done in your town—whether it is being done well, and by whom. No town should be spared intelligent inquiry on this question. Some citizens of a town in Wisconsin asked that question and found the job was left to the police. The animals were taken to the dump and shot. An awful lot got away wounded. It wasn't the fault of the police department. They were simply working with what the community gave them to work with, their guns. If you care about animals, then care about this. Questions should be asked and accurate answers found in every community in America. Only then will we phase out animal abuses perpetuated in the name of humane treatment.

Euthanasia, when the elected course of a pet owner, can be a blessing at those times when a pet has grown too old to keep, or has become grievously ill. How do you handle this situation? What do you tell the children? To begin with, you tell them the truth. One of the nice things about being a nonhuman animal is that you do not have to suffer the terrible indignity of a hopeless life. An animal whose active life has passed can be given merciful sleep, as can an animal afflicted by disease or trauma. The job should be done by a veterinarian, and the hardier of pet owners insist on being present when it is done. The rapid overdose of drugs is painless and so quick there is not time enough for the animal to be afraid.

Of course, it is sad when a pet must die. Death is never a pleasant thing, and pets do lead relatively short lives. Gerbils, hamsters, mice may live only a few years. Some dogs, like Great Danes and Bulldogs, may make ten, smaller dogs may make fifteen, and occasionally, a cat will reach twenty. But it is usually less than that. If a child is involved, I see nothing wrong in invoking whatever religious beliefs you hold in your family. I see nothing sacrilegious about saying that a favorite pet has gone to heaven. (If there is a heaven, I'll bet you a few pets I have known are there.) Then, a commonly asked question is How soon should the pet be replaced? There is no answer to that. Some people feel that time should pass lest the child decide that loved ones can be replaced like broken toys; others feel an immediate replacement is in order to take the child's mind off the loss. It usually depends on a number of things, especially the child. Children are, by the way, often better about these things than adults. They have mechanisms to handle them. The loss of a pet is a small, private family sorrow. Perhaps one value of losing a pet is that it helps the child to handle pain. That could make things easier some inevitable day in the future.

. . . And If You Cannot Keep a Pet: It sometimes happens that, after years of love and companionship, one cannot keep a pet. Personal illness, a death in the family, a change in fortunes, there are a thousand valid reasons that can precipitate the crisis: what to do with the dog or cat we can no longer manage. The best thing to do, obviously, is to find a new home. I do believe that many more dogs and cats would end up in good new homes if people simply tried harder. If a dog or a cat has given you the better part of a lifetime of love, isn't that animal worth a day of your time?

Start in the morning and call everyone you know. Start with family and friends and work outward to acquaintances, even to tradesmen with whom you do business, such as the barber or beauty-shop operator. If you have the time, get the shops you patronize to post signs. If you have snapshots of the pet, make them part of the signs. Ask your veterinarian for help; ask everyone you know. Elderly people often prefer an older pet, one that won't be likely to outlive them and is already housebroken and well mannered. The volunteer adoption agencies work this way. They find scores of homes, so why can't you? Call a local newspaper or radio personality and explain your plight. Often, they will help with a picture, story, or announcement. Put yourself into it. You owe your pet that much at least.

If all of that is not possible, if you have been hit hard by changes and urgencies as sometimes arise in our lives, then seek a shelter that does work at finding new homes. Check out all such shelters—look around very carefully, or get someone who loves you to do it for you. Don't drop your pet off at a pound and turn your back. There are so many animals simply tossed aside like that, few of them find new homes. But even the pound is better than abandoning your pet when you move away. That you must never do.

If worse comes to worst, then there is the ultimate solution—unpleasant, unhappy, but at times necessary. If all else fails, see your veterinarian and have your pet put to sleep with an injection. Accept no other method than that. It isn't expensive unless you call for cremation or other really unnecessary frills. There are times for some people when this problem becomes a crushing reality. If that happens, think of the animal first, of what is best for your friend.

Traveling with Pets: It would be a blessing if more animal owners knew something about the art of traveling with their pets. What are some of the precautions pet owners should take? First, all shots should be up to date, including rabies. Second, I would strongly urge heartworm prophylaxis. Discuss it with your veterinarian; I think he will agree. And, if your pet is a bitch, she will be a lot easier to be with on the road if she has been spayed.

Don't count on finding your pet's favorite food everywhere you go; carry a good supply and also have a water dish at hand at all times. Be certain—and this is most important—that the places you plan to visit allow pets. That includes motels and hotels, parks, forests, reserves, and monuments. A lot of people get turned away, much to their chagrin, when they reach their destination and find they can't take their pet in with them. This often results in animals being left locked in cars, and in summer that can mean agony and death. Some smaller dogs can die of heat prostration in as little as ten minutes. People don't like leaving windows ajar in strange and often unattended parking lots. So before you leave on a trip, you should lay out your entire travel plan and be certain about whether you should take along your pet at all.

When on the road, keep your pet under control. In the case of a dog, that means, almost always, keeping it on a leash. It may not understand local hazards, such as snakes and poisons. Beware in livestock country that there aren't coyote-getters or traps or other insane devices where you go to exercise your friend. Thousands of pets have been killed that way. I would also advise that your dog be tattooed and registered with the National Dog Registry before you hit the road. It is often your only hope in the event of an unexpected separation in strange territory.

One last thing: Make sure you have room in the car for your pet before taking it along. That goes not only for your cat and your dog, but also for your garter snake, hamster, and canary.

Shipping Your Pet: There are times when there is no alternative to crating your cat or dog and shipping it. An unavoidable and unmeasurable degree of hazard goes with entrusting your pet to a freight-handling facility, but there are things you can do to minimize the danger.

Avoid shipping in seasons of extreme heat and cold. Obviously, if you ship your dog to an airport in upstate New York or North Dakota when the temperature there may be way below zero, you are adding an element of risk. A crate inadvertently left on a handcart or not pulled into a building is one thing when it is 60 degrees outside and quite another when it is 30 below. The same, of course, goes for extreme heat. Just as you shouldn't ship to North Dakota in December, try not to ship to Texas and Arizona in July and August. A crate left in the sun for even a few minutes will turn into an oven when it is 105 degrees in the shade.

Take all possible steps to avoid plane changes. That is a danger spot, the off-loading and waiting for the connecting flight. That is when a crate can go astray and not be relocated before a dog or cat is dead or dying. It is not always possible to get a through flight, but when they are available they should be utilized.

The crate used for shipping an animal should be in good condition and be large enough to allow the animal at least freedom to move naturally. There should be no sharp or projecting points or edges. The crates available from the airlines themselves are probably the best for most uses.

Always be in telephone contact with the parties on the receiving end. It is unwise to have the animal trucked by a carrier at the far end. Much better is to have someone you know and trust meet the plane and get the animal away as quickly as possible. If a trucker is used, he should have instructions to call you as soon as he has collected the animal, and you should have his name and telephone number.

You should be certain that your veterinarian has seen the animal prior to shipment and that it has all the necessary protection, including heartworm and rabies. It is not a good idea to tranquilize animals for shipment because they then lose the ability to adjust their body temperature, and if there is a drop in compartment temperature aboard the aircraft, the animal can be severely stressed. As with all aspects of pet owning, when you ship an animal the key to success and to the humane treatment of the animal is common sense and the desire to be kind.

The Eagle and the Boy: I am always interested in stories that reflect the many facets of the relationship between man and animal. There is one from California that tells us something, I believe.

A boy was very ill. He was sixteen and severely disturbed; he was regressing, slipping back toward his own fetal state. He could not or would not speak, he had to be fed, he was a zombie, a robot. They did notice one thing, though—they noticed that they could get eye movement when they showed him pictures of birds. Just birds. He would move his eyes to follow a picture. Nothing else could crack the shell he had built around himself.

The boy's story was told to a friend of mine by the name of Ralph Helfer. Ralph trains animals for the movies, and the boy was brought to his animal compound. They stood him in front of a cage where a trained Golden Eagle was kept. He followed the bird with his eyes and he also spoke, single words, but the first he had in six months. They put a leather gauntlet on him and brought the eagle to his arm. The poor bedeviled kid stood there with an eagle perched on his arm, and he smiled. No one could remember how long it had been since that had happened. There was a greenhouse at the hospital where the boy was kept, and the eagle was eventually moved there for the boy to care for, the boy who weeks before could not feed himself or see to his own bodily functions. He began going to the compound and helping with the care of the other animals, and he cared for his eagle. Within six months, the boy was back in public school, and I understand that he and his eagle (the bird is now his) are doing just fine.

I don't know who understands all this. I have had other reports about cases where severely alienated, almost totally isolated people were finally able to bridge back into the real world with the help of an animal. Sometimes it is a dog, sometimes a cat, sometimes the quieting effect of fish moving through the liquid world of the aquarium. And sometimes it takes a mighty tiger of the skies, a Golden Eagle, to gently lift a dying sixteen-year-old kid and carry him back to the world of the living. Maybe I'll understand it someday, but in the meantime, it helps me to understand even better the things I like to think I stand for, the things I do and believe in.

2

DOGS IN GENERAL

Picking a Breed of Dog: What kind of a dog should a person or family get? A number of considerations apply, whether you are seeking a specialty breeder and buying a purebred dog, or going to the pound and saving a random-bred animal from the euthanasia room. What do you want in a dog? Companionship? If so, at what level: a big thumper to run beside you in the woods and fields, or a snug little cushion-sitter? There is a world of difference between maintaining a Yorkshire Terrier and maintaining a Labrador Retriever, yet both are superb companion animals. Is your life sedentary or are you very active? Would you like tossing a ball to a wildly cavorting Terrier, or would you want a Basset Hound that will sit by your side while you stare at the fire and sip your port?

The first consideration, then, is need. What are your needs? Be very honest with yourself. Do you want a great lumbering teddy-bear dog, or do you want a dog that will be a child in your home and never grow up? That is what the Toys are, as well as some other breeds, like the Boston Terrier—eternal children. Is the dog for your children as well, or perhaps primarily? If so, how old are your kids and how well behaved? Do they need a Newfoundland that can hold its own against a thundering herd of kids, or are your kids basically gentle and well controlled, so that a Whippet might do? Before anything else, carefully and honestly analyze your life-style and determine what you really are going to expect of the dog you get. Once you have done that, you are in a position to analyze the other factors: size, coat-care needs, exercise requirements, cost, and fashionability, all real factors, but none more important than the basic questions we have just asked.

Sit down with your family, look them over (and have them look you over, too), and decide what you are going to ask this dog to be. Purebred or random-bred, there is a dog for you, but before you know him, you have to know yourself.

Having decided what you want a dog to be, the role it is to play in your home, let's turn next to the question of size. Dogs range from tiny Toys, like the Chihuahua and the smaller Yorkshire Terriers; through the Boston Terriers and smaller Spaniels; through the medium-sized, like the Basset and the Bulldog; to the large-sized, such as the Retrievers, Setters, and Working breeds, like Boxers and Shepherds; all the way to the giants, like the Bullmastiff; and up to the Irish Wolfhound. That is an enormous range. A St. Bernard or a Wolfhound can weigh close to eighty times as much as a Yorkshire Terrier. But size is not a factor to be taken alone, because size may not tell you the animal's exercise requirements. A small Fox Terrier needs more running than a Mastiff. These two things must work together, size and exercise.

Be honest with yourself. How much room can you spare? How much trouble will you have stepping over and around a Great Dane that is spread out across your living room, and how much exercise are you going to want to give your pet? And what kind of exercise? A German Shepherd and a Mastiff will want to be walked several miles a day. It will be good for both of you. A Golden Retriever is going to want to fetch, winter and summer, especially from water. A Whippet is going to want to really run, and an Italian Greyhound is going to want to sit home and pose. What kind of attention can you give?

Don't get a dog that is so big it will be in the way and eventually be resented, and don't get a dog that will go stir crazy with the kind of life-style to which it will have to accommodate itself. You can't count on opening the door and having the dog exercise itself. That is not exercise, it is dogicide. Dogs should not be allowed to wander. There are exceptions, of course. On a farm or ranch you don't have to leash your dog and walk it around the back forty, but in the city you certainly need a leash, in the suburbs it is usually required, and it is even necessary in many rural areas where there are highways. In most situations, then, the exercise your dog gets will be up to you and other members of the family. How much and what kind can you provide?

How about the dog's coat? Some people really like to fuss over their pet, but many more don't, and before buying a dog you should decide where you stand on this matter. Of course, you can always get a dog whose coat needs a lot of care and then give out the contract. Many grooming services pick up and deliver, so all you have to do is pay the bill. Your dog is picked up at the door, and then brought back all shiny and renewed. That can be expensive, anywhere from ten dollars a time to almost fifty dollars. It depends on where you live and what you want in the way of services.

If you are going to groom your dog yourself, be sure you want to undertake the learning and the equipment-buying that goes with it. Take, for example, a Poodle. It needs more than brushing. There is trimming and pulling and designing. It is a hobby in itself, if it is to be done well and if that Poodle is to look smashing at all times. With other breeds, Spaniels and Setters for instance, brushing is the thing. They have feathers on their legs, and their ears are subject to terrible tangles. They really do have to be brushed very often, vigorously, too, and not just for a minute or so. Is that what you want to do with your dog? The shorter-haired dogs, those with hard, close coats, need a quick going-over from time to time, but that is nothing compared to what we have been talking about. A sloppy dog is like a sloppy house, an unmade bed, a soiled rug, a spot on your tie or bib—it reflects on you. In this case, though, it can also reflect on the dog, for it is getting into a worse mess all the time you are ignoring its coat. If you are thinking of your next dog, or your first dog, be honest with yourself. How much coat care do you want to give it? Bloodhounds, Boston Terriers, and Bulldogs need almost none; the Borzoi, the Cocker Spaniel, and the Schnauzer need a lot. Pick your place in that spectrum and keep it in mind. It is a very important factor in picking your breed.

There are a number of other factors for you to consider. No doubt many people consider style important when they select a dog, and that is not all bad. There is some hazard, though, in selecting a stylish breed (very often one that won at Westminster last time around). You may pay a great deal more for a fine puppy than you have to. Supply and demand works with pets, too. You will also run the risk of getting an inferior example of a breed. When a dog breed shows signs of becoming a fad (in the recent past this has included German Shepherds, Boston Terriers, Cocker Spaniels, Boxers, Poodles, and a number of others), the unscrupulous breeders begin mass-producing examples by crossing brothers and sisters, mothers and sons, fathers and daughters, anything to get more puppies off to the puppy shops. It is then more important than ever that you buy from the highly reputable specialty breeder *only*—that is, the breeder who has long been a specialist with that breed, who cares about that one breed more than any other; enough, in fact, to devote his life to it.

Be sure, too, that fashion isn't the only thing you are looking for. You can redecorate a living room, throw

out a suit or frock, but an animal is a living creature
and is with you from ten to fifteen years. Make certain
you really want a sleek and wonderful sight Hound like
the Afghan, and not that you just think it will make you
look smart at the top end of a leash. That is no basis
for inviting an animal into the family or for making a
long-term commitment. There are over 120 breeds and
you should look at a good many of them before making
a decision. Buying a dog you are not going to cherish
for as long as it lives is both silly and cruel. Style is
fine, fashion is fine, but they are no bases for anything
meaningful. By definition, fashion and style are frivo-
lous pastimes. A pet is not.

The Groups of Dogs: The groups to which the American Kennel Club assigns breeds for purposes of competition number six for recognized breeds, plus a miscellaneous class for breeds not yet accorded full
recognition. The six basic classes are the Sporting Dogs,
the Hounds, the Working Dogs, the Terriers, the Toys,
and the Non-Sporting Dogs.

There are twenty-four breeds of Sporting Dogs.
These include the Setters, the Spaniels, the Pointers,
and the Retrievers, animals of that pattern and use.
The Hounds number nineteen and include both sight
Hounds—Borzoi, Wolfhound, Whippet, Greyhound—
and scent Hounds, like the Beagle, Basset, and Bloodhound. The Dachshund, by the way, is a Hound, and
so is the Basenji. The Working Dogs number thirty and
include the obvious ones like the Collie, the German
Shepherd, and the sled dogs, as well as a few mild
surprises like the Great Dane and the Corgis. The Boxer,
too, is a Working Dog.

There are twenty-two Terriers, including the Miniature Schnauzer (the Standard Schnauzer belongs back

there with the Working Dogs). The Toys number seventeen and include the Miniature Pinscher (the big variety is, again, a Working Dog), the Pug, and the Yorkshire Terrier. Note the Yorkie is not in the Terrier group, but with the Toys. The Shih Tzu is a Toy, as are the Manchester Terrier and the English Toy Spaniel. You can't always trust that last name. The Japanese Spaniel is a Toy, whereas most Spaniels are Sporting Dogs. The sixth group is the Non-Sporting Dogs. It is a catchall for eleven breeds so diverse we had better name them all: they are the Boston Terrier, Tibetan Terrier, English Bulldog, Chow Chow, Dalmatian, French Bulldog, Bichon Frise, Keeshond, Lhasa Apso, Poodle, and Schipperke. Note that the Toy Poodle is a Toy; why the French Bulldog should not be one, too, since the Pug is, is a little puzzling.

Anyway, those are the American Kennel Club groupings, and in a dog show for mixed breeds, once a dog or bitch has taken best in breed, it goes for best in group. Then the best in each group is put up, six dogs competing for best in show.

The Sporting Breeds: There are twenty-four Sporting Dog breeds. They include the Spaniels, the Retrievers, and the Pointers, and such special dogs as the Vizsla, the Weimaraner, and the Wirehaired Pointing Griffon; and let's not forget the Setters. A number of people feel that three of the greatest dogs of all time are the Gordon Setter, the Labrador, and the Golden Retriever, great from the standpoints of brains, personality, and reliability. Of course the fanciers of the Working Dogs, animals like the Collie, the Husky, the St. Bernard, and the Newfoundland, might not agree, but they would agree there is something special in these Sporting animals. Some of them have been around for quite a while, but as a group they are generally more recently evolved than some of the other classes. There has been a great deal of crossing to achieve the twenty-four we know today. The Spaniels reached their peak of development in the British Isles, but they originated, as their name implies, in Spain. France and Germany contributed to the Sporting group. The Retrievers carry Canadian blood, although much of their development took place in the British Isles. Over the centuries, Spaniel blood and Retriever blood have been crossed, and there is a great deal of each in the other. Proof of this can be seen in the English Setter. In the sixteenth century, he was called "the Spaniel."

There apparently is some Hound and Terrier in the Sporting bloodlines as well, for the men who wanted the best of all possible dogs in the field drew upon the entire dog world for desirable characteristics. What characterizes a Sporting Dog? Well, intelligence, certainly, and tenacity. These dogs aren't always the fastest learners, but they are among the slowest forgetters. Once a dog of this group knows what is expected of him, he never forgets. It grows in him like bone and muscle. Do the Spaniels, Setters, Pointers, and Retrievers make good pets? Certainly, although they are outdoor dogs, and I hate to see them cooped up. These are dogs that were meant to move, meant to work, meant to know the bite of clean, cool air. They are friends to run with, to take afield, and with whom you can share the world of nature. [For individual descriptions of the most popular Sporting breeds, see pages 85 to 98.]

The Hounds: There are nineteen Hounds recognized by the American Kennel Club today, and they have long served man well.

The Hounds vary tremendously in style and manner, including dogs as different as the Dachshund and the Irish Wolfhound (there you have shoulder heights ranging from five to thirty-three inches), as different as the Basset and the Whippet, and I promise you, when you speak of the Basset and the Whippet, you are speaking of a difference. The Hounds have served man in both sporting and working capacities, although they are rated as neither Working nor Sporting Dogs, and their origins are lost far, far back in the mists of the earliest civilizations. The Borzoi, one of the most magnificent of the coursing Hounds, was derived from stock already four thousand years old when imported into Russia by noblemen of estimable taste. The Dachshund, the shortest of the Hounds by a wide margin, arose in Germany in the seventeenth century and was used to go to earth after badger. He was bigger then than now.

There are two kinds of Hounds basically, the sight Hounds and the scent Hounds. The Afghan, the Borzoi or Russian Wolfhound, the Irish Wolfhound, the Greyhound, and the Whippet are classic examples of sight Hounds. They course animals, but not by scent. They have sharp eyesight, great speed, and enormous endurance. They can wind a wolf. Scent Hounds include the Bloodhound, the Basset, the Beagle, the Coonhound, that manner of beast. Their sense of smell and their stick-to-it-iveness are nothing less than phenomenal, especially in the case of the Bloodhound. As one man once said, "A Bloodhound can smell what you're thinking." The scent Hounds have none of the sight Hounds' swift grace, but they are handsome and special in their own way.

Because some of the Hounds have been used for tracking outlaws, they have gotten themselves bad names. They are fine dogs, fine pets, and usually excellent with children. The bigger coursing dogs—magnificent statuesque creatures like the Borzoi, the Irish Wolfhound, and the Scottish Deerhound—belong where there is open land. These animals should move if they are to be healthy and realize their full potential. You have a wide choice if you decide to look at the Hounds. Nineteen distinctly different styles, designs, and personalities are yours for the asking. [For individual descriptions of the most popular Hound breeds, see pages 98 to 111.]

The Working Breeds: They have helped man build his world of farm and city. They have been essential to man's progress.

We recognize thirty breeds of Working Dogs. Included are the sled dogs (the Siberian Husky, the Alaskan Malamute, and the Samoyed), the herding dogs, the Belgian and English sheepdogs, the Collies, the Puli, and the Shetland Sheepdog, among others. Also included are the police and military dogs, German Shepherd, Doberman Pinscher—that manner of beast that has served as watchdog and patrol dog. These are all Working breeds. Today they are largely pets, although the animals that guide the blind are often from this group, as are those on patrol in warehouses and military installations.

We don't use dogs as beasts of burden in America, but we still cherish beasts like the Mastiff, the Dane, and the Boxer. We also like the St. Bernard (he's still one of the most popular dogs in America), although he doesn't still run around with a keg of brandy hanging from his neck, worse luck! The Corgis are among the Working Dogs, for they were originally farm animals, cattle dogs very adept at nipping heels. The Standard Schnauzer is in the group too, for it too was a cattle driver that doubled in brass as a ratter. Since dogs have been used by agriculturists and husbandrymen for centuries, many of our Working Dogs date far back in history. The Pembroke Corgi may go back to the Celts of 1200 B.C., the Great Pyrenees back almost four thousand years to the lands of Asia Minor. The Great Dane, a German breed, may trace back to Greco-Roman times to a dog we refer to as the Molossian dog. The Tiger dog of Egypt may have been his ancestor. So, the Working breeds come by their traits naturally.

It is hard to imagine how man could have developed socially as he did without the help of these dogs. They made sheep, goat, and cattle herding possible. We can suppose it would have been possible without dogs, but there would have been less time for poetry and music and just plain musing. The dog gave man his first leisure. We will never know the whole history of man and dog, although we have been wondering about it for centuries. One thing we have always known and should always know is that we are much indebted to the dog, a creature we often treat badly indeed. [For individual descriptions of the most popular Working breeds, see pages 111 to 127.]

The Terriers: The breeds of dogs known as Terriers are some of the toughest and roughest little characters in the world of canine personalities.

They run from *A* to *W*, from Airedale to West Highland White Terrier, and their spunk has no limit. The Terriers' name comes from the Latin *terra,* which means "earth," and that tells us something about these animals. They were earth dogs designed—literally designed by genetic engineering—to work on farms and estates ferreting out rats and other rodents. Today they are rarely anything but pets, and wonderful pets they are. Although they include the smaller Schnauzer, a German breed, the group can rightly be considered a development of the British Isles. Just a quick rundown of some of the breed names makes this point clear enough: Bedlington, Cairn, Dandie Dinmont, Irish, Kerry Blue, Lakeland, Manchester, Norwich, Scottish, Sealyham, Skye, Staffordshire Bull, Welsh, and West Highland White. Put the word Terrier after each of those names and you have most of the Terrier breeds. (The Tibetan Terrier, so called, is not truly a Terrier.) As domestic animals go, the Terriers are not very old. Most originated in the 1800s, a few in the 1700s. Very few can trace their history back further than two hundred years. We know what little we know of the Terriers' ancestral forms because artists very often painted their patrons in the company of their animals, and a visit to any art museum will reveal many of today's dogs in earlier forms.

No doubt many Terrier breeds developed in the last two centuries have since passed out of existence. Some may never even have been given a name, and few reached breed status. Farmers and estate owners took their Sporting Dogs and bred them to a whole wide variety of dogs, including fiery little mutts that roamed the England of Charles Dickens. From those crosses, records of which we do not have, came the tough little ratters, and some larger dogs, too, that have come down to us as Terriers. But not all Terriers are small. The Airedale can weigh fifty pounds, the Bull Terrier, a very tough fighting dog, can weigh sixty. The beautiful Kerry Blue, a breed that belongs in the hands of a really good handler, can stand almost twenty inches at the shoulder. The Terriers are among the Western world's favorite pets. Many of the top forty dog breeds are Terriers. The Boston Terrier and the Yorkshire are also in the top forty, but they are not Terrier breeds despite their names. The Boston is a Non-Sporting Dog and the Yorkie is a Toy. Everyone loves the Terriers, but not everyone should own one. They have strong personalities and belong in the hands of people who are willing to work at being a master. [For individual descriptions of the most popular Terrier breeds, see pages 127 to 134.]

The Toy Breeds: There are seventeen breeds of dogs shown as Toy breeds in this country. They are a group that fulfills a very special purpose, for the Toys are not dogs that herd, or retrieve, or patrol, or pull carts. They are the breeds that love. That is what they were bred for, to give and get an extraordinary amount of love. They are generally spoiled rotten. That tends to be built in.

The Toy Poodle, the Chihuahua, and the Pekingese are probably the best known of the Toys. The Yorkshire Terrier, the Pug, and the Pomeranian are up there in popularity, too. The Affenpinscher and Brussels Griffon are less known in this country, and the English Toy Spaniel will almost certainly become more popular as time passes. The Italian Greyhound that looks rather like a small Whippet is one of the sweetest of all Toys, while the Japanese Spaniel and the Maltese are very cute and make favorite cuddling animals. The Manchester Terrier in full size is shown as a Terrier, but there is a Toy Manchester, too, and also a Miniature Pinscher, known affectionately as the Minipin to its fanciers. The Papillon or Butterfly Dog is a lovely little creature with enormous ears that give it its name. The Shih Tzu and the Silky Terrier, the latter an Australian invention, are growing rapidly in popularity.

The Toys, all of them, represent a certain honesty on the part of their owners. They are a clear statement that a need was discerned and met. The Toys are what I like to call *neotonous*, they never grow up. They remain children all of their lives and are meant to be fussed over. A number of the Toys are coated dogs—that is, animals with elaborate coats—and that adds to the task of caring for them and thereby the joy of having them.

Some Toys are fine with children and some tend to be jealous and must be the only child in the family. It tends to vary from individual to individual as much as from breed to breed. Some of the Toys have been bred down to absolutely astounding sizes—a couple of pounds in the case of the tiny Yorkshire Terriers. That is not always healthy for the dog. When Toy breeds get too small, most veterinarians advise against breeding them.

The Toys are amazing little creatures, very often giant dogs that have been all squished down into tiny bodies. When you see someone with a Toy, you will know he or she is essentially honest. This person is not afraid to be known as someone who really does love dogs, for that is what the Toys are all about. [For individual descriptions of the most popular Toy breeds, see pages 134 to 145.]

The Non-Sporting Breeds: The grouping is arbitrary. There are eleven breeds in it and some of them were once hunting dogs. Today they are companions.

The Non-Sporting breeds are the Bichon Frise, Boston Terrier, English Bulldog, Chow Chow, Dalmatian, French Bulldog, Keeshond, Lhasa Apso, Poodle, Tibetan Terrier, and Schipperke. That includes a few of my favorite breeds and one of my least favorite of all (which one, I'll keep a secret). Because this grouping is so arbitrary, a catchall, there is little that can be said about it as a group. After all, what do the Poodle and the Dalmatian, or the English Bulldog and the Chow Chow have in common? Not much, I promise you, except a leg in each corner and a smeller up front. Just look at the geographical spread. The Boston Terrier is an American breed. The Bulldog is English, the Chow Chow is Chinese, the Dalmatian is Dalmatian, the French Bulldog is, not at all surprisingly, French, the Keeshond is Dutch, the Tibetan Terrier and the Lhasa Apso are Tibetan, the Poodle is German, and the Schipperke is Flemish/Belgian.

As for quality in the home, these are companion dogs. That is what their life today is all about. The Poodle, once a water retriever, is now a companion dog, as is the Boston Terrier, who was bred as such originally. The Chow Chows were almost certainly hunting dogs in China. I just can't resist saying something about the English Bulldog. We have one. Her name is Glynnis and we bought her in London. As my wife says, she is just another pretty face. If you want a dog that makes you smile every time it looks at you, this is a Non-Sporting breed to consider. The fact that the breed was once developed to fight bulls has nothing to do with their habits today. While they aren't good at chasing a coach like their fellow Non-Sporting breed, the Dalmatian, they do have their uses, mostly having to do with making you feel all warm and foolish inside, but, why not?

If you are thinking of adding a dog to your collection, take a look at the Non-Sporting breeds. At least ten of them make lovely additions to any family. The eleventh? That's my secret. [For individual descriptions of the most popular Non-Sporting breeds, see pages 145 to 154.]

The Miscellaneous-Class Breeds: There is a group of dogs not shown in America among the recognized

breeds but that still have their following: the miscellaneous-class breeds. These breeds may one day have
the recognition 123 other breeds already have in the
American Kennel Club. If their fanciers had their way,
they would be recognized now. Among these breeds of
future show rings is the Australian Cattle Dog, also
known as the Blue Cattle Dog. As his name implies, he
is a working dog, a herder; they say he is part Collie,
part Kelpie, and part Wild Dingo. The Australian
Kelpie, also known as the Barb, is included. He has the
look of the German Shepherd about him. The Border
Collie has many followers and fans and is well known
in the British Isles and will one day be recognized here
as well. Another breed is the pretty little Cavalier King
Charles Spaniel. That is his full name, not a description
—Cavalier King Charles Spaniel. He is a kind of reconstructed English Toy Spaniel and has lots of fans already.

The Ibizan Hound is from Spain. He looks like Anubis, the watchdog of the dead from ancient Egyptian
tombs, and that is probably in line with his origin. He
is a sleek, exotic-looking creature and not often seen in
America. One breed is just over eighty years old, the
Miniature Bull Terrier, and he looks like what his name
suggests. From Italy, and often called the Italian
Pointer, is the Spinone Italiano, a nice-looking dog. I
predict he will develop a big following in the years
ahead. He is the all-purpose hunting dog of Italy, is
highly efficient, and was developed over several centuries in the Piemonte section of northwestern Italy.
He has a keen look about him, Those are the miscellaneous breeds and some licensed shows do offer a class
for them. One day they will each undoubtedly be assigned to one of the regular AKC groupings, but in the
meantime, like all breeds, they have to show a standard
and a following worthy of recognition.

Puppy Mills: They are a tragedy of our times—they are often filthy, often illegal on one or many counts, and they are frequently cruel. Supported by our ignorance, they are mass-producing living creatures.

A professional dog breeder is a man or woman who devotes his or her life to the improvement of a breed of dog—perhaps two breeds, seldom more than that. A puppy mill is a wholesale mass-production operation turning out highly questionable dogs for pet shops. One such operator advertises in a trade journal that he has sixty-four breeds of dogs for sale. How, we must ask, does a man devote his life to improving the standards of sixty-four breeds? Many puppy mills are cruel, extremely cruel—and the Humane Society of the United States in Washington, D.C., is forever answering complaints by putting its investigators on the road. The files they have amassed are damning indeed to these wholesale breeders. If you anticipate buying a purebred dog, buy *only* from a professional breeder whose premises you visit. Allow no one to come between you and the people who bred the dog—see their kennels, see their adult dogs, including the parents of the puppy you are thinking of buying. And see their credentials. Puppy mills are frequently rackets, and the pet shops who handle their product often know less than nothing about the dogs they offer for sale. They order by phone and receive the puppies, often sick and sometimes dead, in orange crates or worse. They brush them up, put them in the window, and make extravagant claims as to their lineage and quality. Buy from a breeder—care enough about the dog in your future to learn something about its past. Check with the American Kennel Club in New York if you want to find a listing of qualified breeders near you. Squeeze out the puppy mill—it is a blight and a sorrow.

Random-Bred Dogs: There are many more random-bred dogs in America than purebred dogs, and a lot of misconceptions about them. Let's profile the all-American mutt. First, he or she—let's call it she here—she is a lover. No one but God above knows what is in her or where or how she came into being, but you saw her in a shelter and made a five-dollar contribution, and now she is yours. You are a responsible person, so she has been spayed and has had all her shots. Now she wants your love and little more. (All the other things she has to have will be automatic if you love her.) She requires the same food, exactly, required by purebred dogs of her age, although you may not know how much bone you have to build, as you would with, say, a Bloodhound or Yorkshire Terrier. A random-bred animal may weigh twenty pounds when full-grown or she may weigh forty. You really can't tell by her paws. Watch your little random-bred's diet and give her plenty of bone meal and vitamin supplements. Let your veterinarian guide you in that.

What else? Parasites? Likely to be loaded. That, too, must be seen to. And watch for kennel cough. It is often found in puppies from the pound. Don't let her wander. You can't trust her road sense, and she will look as sad dead by the curb as would a Schnauzer or any other purebred dog. Your little random-bred friend needs as much shelter as a purebred animal and as many checkups at her own doctor's clinic.

How about intelligence? Is it true that she will be smarter than a purebred dog? Well, more intelligent than some, but probably no more so than those breeds already known for their brains—Retrievers and Poodles, for example. Will she live long? Probably, if you give her the food and care she deserves. Will she return your love if you give it freely? You better believe it.

What to Look for in a Puppy: What do you look for when you buy a puppy? There is that basic appeal, of course: you could call it charisma. But beyond that personal reaction, or perhaps *interaction* would be a better word, there are other things. Brightness and alertness, responsiveness, are the first signs to look for. A puppy that doesn't feel well—and puppies, like small children, react instantly to infection—will not be bright and responsive. It will be lethargic. Also like children, puppies play hard and then, when they are tired, they collapse to recharge their batteries. You should see a puppy over a period of hours or on different days at different times of the day to judge that properly.

A puppy should feel and smell warm and sweet. Its skin should be loose and go back into shape immediately after being pulled into a bunch. The coat should not be dry or brittle, and the eyes should be clear and bright. The nose should also be clear, without sign of discharge. The belly should be round and solid and without any unusual swellings such as might be caused by an umbilical hernia. A puppy should like to be handled and should not react with fear when gently stroked or lifted. A pup that tries to devour your nose and pull your hair out by the roots is showing good healthy puppy signs.

If the dog is to be a purebred, it is a very good idea to know the standards of the breed you are considering, for although a puppy will not show you very much beyond general appearance before it is four to six months old, you can get an idea of markings and color. That can be important in some breeds. Be sure to read the breed description carefully, for some breeds don't get their adult color until they approach maturity. The idea is to know what the breed is supposed to look like.

It is very important, if you can work it out, to see the parents of the puppy, or other more mature dogs from that match from an earlier litter. If the dog is a random-bred animal, the same general rules apply and are just as important, except the color and markings; the variations on any single theme are endless.

What you should look for in a puppy also has a great deal to do with what you want in a dog. It is one thing to buy a companion for your kids and another to seek the greatest Whippet or Papillon or Bloodhound in the show world. But no matter what you want the dog to be, the first thing you must have is a healthy puppy. Take the time to look. It will pay off in a lot of happy years to follow.

Shots for Your Dog: Just what shots your puppy should have and when they should be given are decisions to be made by a competent veterinarian. They are basic elements in responsible pet care.

Canine distemper, with its fifty percent death rate, is the chief concern. Initially, the puppy is protected by colostrum or "first milk" immunization gained by nursing. Very quickly, though, that barrier is lost and the puppy depends on the protection your veterinarian can give it. The exact age when that natural protection is lost is not known, so modified live-virus is usually administered at six, nine, and twelve weeks of age. Often a permanent shot is given at nine months with yearly boosters from then on. Obviously, it is important for your dog to be seen by a veterinarian as early as possible. He may feel, after examining the puppy and possibly its mother, that it is advisable to start the protection earlier than at six weeks. It is for him to decide.

Infectious canine hepatitis, a viral disease like distemper, is difficult to diagnose. It is not transmittable to man, but it can be fatal in about ten percent of cases in dogs. Shots are given along with the distemper immunization.

Leptospirosis is an infectious disease of both man and animal. It is passed along through urine, and eight hundred human cases have been reported in one recent decade. Although not exactly an epidemic, such a toll is not to be overlooked. A vaccine is available and is usually given at the same time as distemper and infectious canine hepatitis shots.

Some veterinarians prefer to give shots for parainfluenza virus. It offers protection against an infection known as kennel cough. The final shot course for us to consider is the one given to prevent the disease with one-hundred-percent fatality—rabies. It is too often overlooked. It is true that we may see only two to three hundred canine cases a year in this country, but the disease is so infectious, so violent, and so very deadly that no dog should be without protection. That protection is for your family as well. It is especially important that dogs that are going to travel and dogs that are turned loose in the field where they might encounter wildlife be inoculated. A dog, once it has its shots, should carry a tag on its collar. It is provided automatically by your veterinarian. If, for some reason, your dog should ever bite anyone, it could mean its life or death to have had those shots.

The immunization of dogs against the most important infectious diseases is clearly the responsibility of the owners of those animals. There are no mysteries to any of this. It is something your veterinarian does hundreds of times a month. It is something that should not be put off even for a day.

Your Pup's First Night: If there is ever a time when humane instincts and a full measure of common sense are required, it is on the day when a new pet checks in to become a member of the family.

Before you actually bring your new puppy into his new home, try to put yourself into his shoes, or paws. What must it be like for him to face a whole new world of towering strangers and unfamiliar sounds and smells? It isn't easy, and to the babylike nervous system of a puppy, it can be downright shocking. Some puppies, of course, take it much better than others, but most puppies, like human babies, are frightened or at least confused by loud noises. When a puppy hears something new, it has to sort it out, and if six squealing kids and adults are all pulling at it and shouting at the same time, it will be at a loss and may respond with fear. In a word, *quiet*. Take it soft and easy. Keep it all low key. It should be obvious that a tug-of-war isn't the best nerve tonic, especially if you are the rope! Give the poor creature a chance.

Smells mean a lot to all but the youngest puppy, so let the little stranger wander around and sniff, particularly if it is a home where there are or have been other animals. Animal smells will intrigue and confuse him. Let him come to you, to each member of the family in turn. Try to discourage your children's natural desire to fetch and bring in every friend they have during those first few hours. Again, give the puppy a chance. In the long run, you will find he will settle down better and become established much more quickly if he is allowed those first few hours to find his way into the new world that has been thrust upon him.

As traumatic as his first day may be, his first night with you is potentially even more difficult, especially if he has been removed from his mother and littermates in order to come into your lives. You had better decide from the beginning where he or she is going to sleep. Establish that at the outset and then stick with it. It can be very difficult to change later. The chances are better than good that the puppy is going to end up sleeping on somebody's bed, but if you are the firm type and don't want that, then have a basket ready in a dry, draft-free area with a reasonable temperature. Try giving the puppy a hot-water bottle wrapped in a heavy towel. If he cries, it probably means he is newly away from his mother. Wrap an old-fashioned clock with a nice loud tick in another heavy towel and put that in with him as well. It will remind him of his mother's heartbeat when he cuddled against her at night and will help him settle down. If he continues to cry and your resolve remains firm, then just grin and bear it.

A pet, a living creature brought into your lives on your own decision is a joy, but it is also a responsibility. What is needed is hardly more than good old-fashioned common sense and a feeling of compassion for other creatures that can feel and react. It is surprising how many people are lacking in both. If you want to be listed among the haves and not the have-nots on the day they tally these two qualities, you will have a perfect opportunity to display your wares on your puppy's first day in his new home.

Housebreaking: Of all the little problems that serve to discourage potential dog owners, none is more of an obstacle than housebreaking. It looms as insurmountable for some people, although only in the rarest cases is that dread justified.

The biggest single problem in housebreaking a new pet is communication. A dog wants to please its master and not to be punished. Most dogs will respond very quickly once they understand what it is that is expected of them. Remember, the idea of the valuable oriental rug or the wall-to-wall broadloom you have been waiting years to buy are lost on a dog. He or she can't handle that kind of a concept. The only thing that a dog can understand in all this is that you are pleased or displeased with what he has done. A dog doesn't really understand outside from inside except insofar, once again, as you are happy or unhappy. Clean and unclean are also vague concepts and not available to the dog's mind. Work on the single communication channel of "this makes me happy" and "that makes me angry." Most important, don't get uptight. If you do, so will the dog, and you will have failed to communicate or do anything else constructive.

It is better to praise a dog for doing what has to be done in the right place than to scold him for doing it in the wrong place. That means getting your dog's pattern down and fitting your walks with him into it. Immediately after eating and drinking, the puppy should go outside and then be lavishly praised for being good. It is better if you don't have to paper-train a puppy and then train him for outside. That really is the same as housebreaking the dog twice. If you live in the city, however, your veterinarian may not want a young and vulnerable puppy sniffing around where strange dogs have been. He may require paper-training and later housebreaking. You will find the paper-training the easier of the two tasks, especially if you live in an apartment. It is easier to get a puppy about to err onto a paper in the corner of the kitchen than to get it down the elevator and out into the street.

Be very patient, don't despair, don't panic, and don't brutalize. Make your wishes known and rely on your dog's unvarying desire to please you as your best chance to make your clean-rug dream come true. Dogs are generally much easier to train than children.

Don't Think Puppy, Think Dog: "Don't think puppy, think dog" is good advice on several counts. There is no denying that there are few creatures on earth more appealing than a puppy. The big eyes, the waddle, the curiosity, and the puppy smell; I guess almost everybody loves a puppy. But, remember Ogden Nash's poem? The only trouble with a kitten is that someday it will grow up to be a cat. Anyway, that's close. And a puppy grows up, too, very quickly, in a matter of months.

A lot of people refuse to allow their children to have a dog because they don't want the trouble of housebreaking and replacing chewed shoes, all the things that often can go with a puppy growing up. There is a solution to that problem. It is called Instant Dog. Pounds and shelters are full of Instant Dogs: abandoned, lost, stolen, and then dumped, strays unclaimed, dogs that ran away from the scene of a fire or accident, all trained, instantly ready to serve your family with all the love you can handle. And it is just this kind of animal that so often gets put down because people still think puppy instead of dog.

Instant Dog is an answer, too, for people of reduced activity, and elderly people for whom a puppy would be too much or too long a commitment. Another thing—puppies, Lord love them, grow up to be what they were meant to be, and that may not exactly match what you had in mind. A dog, once matured, is where it is going to be all the rest of its life. Looking at a full-grown but still healthy and vital animal is much more reliable than looking at a puppy's feet and trying to guess how big he will be. Puppies are lovely, nothing is cuter, but it may be a good idea for you or someone you know to think of Instant Dog instead. It can be easier on the nerves, and think of the life you will be saving.

Attack Dogs and Watchdogs: There is more than a little concern in our land about the crime rate, and, unfortunately, many people seem to think that an attack dog is the answer for the average home. Well, they are wrong, and I, for one, am worried about what the results of this trend are going to be.

There is no doubt that a barking dog is one of the best deterrents you can have for burglars, but a barking dog is a far cry from a dog that is trained to attack and even possibly kill. The current fear over crime has brought a number of dangerous fast-buck artists into the dog field who are advertising, selling, and renting attack-trained German Shepherds and Dobermans to private homes. Unsuspecting buyers may believe that you can have an attack dog and a good pet for children all rolled up into one, but they are walking down a dangerous garden path. Attack dogs are not pets. They aren't meant to be. They are like having a loaded gun around the house. Even if the attack dog does treat family members with respect, what about the neighbor's kid that may be wrestling with your youngster on the front lawn and get half his face taken off, or worse?

A dog trained to attack men is a special kind of creature with a special job to do. He doesn't belong in a home, certainly not around children. His world is one of industrial installations, kennels, and highly skilled handlers. A watchdog is something else again. He can be a pet who will bark at strange sounds and strange people. The same breeds can do both jobs. It is their training that makes the difference. Reputable dog dealers and trainers will not sell an attack dog to a private home and will advise strongly against the idea. They know what the product of their training can do when triggered into action. The mere thought of one around kids and delivery boys will make their blood run cold. If you want a watchdog, pick up a breed that suits all of your other family needs, and then get some expert help in training your pet to warn, not to attack. Make certain he is a pet first and a burglar alarm second. And before you buy a dog that has special qualities advertised for it, or before becoming involved with a training school, check with the local breeding and show clubs and the Better Business Bureau. You might even want to talk to the police. You don't want your dog to be one of the many that have to be shot every year because they are inexpertly trained or prove far too much for their owners to handle. I'm not suggesting what breed you should get, just the kind of special training it should have. To steal a line from the Pet Food Institute—and it is a good line to remember—*"the family watchdog should be all bark and no bite."*

Your Dog's Good Manners: Man is a social animal. Our success as individuals depends to a large degree on how successfully we live with other people. Because we keep pets, how our pets behave becomes an extension of our own behavior and a factor in our individual success.

Pet owners are quick to close ranks when there is the slightest sign of antipet sentiment in their community. Any effort to govern or restrict pet ownership is met with an instant outcry. I can understand that. We have six dogs and some horses and ten cats as well. Still, there is that other side. There always is. Many pet owners show total disregard for the rights and sensitivities of other people. A family in an apartment building near me had a Beagle that howled as if the world was coming to an end. Until recently, this family walked their dog at seven in the morning and then went to work. They returned at six in the evening and religiously walked their dog again. Trouble was, from

7:15 A.M. to 6:00 P.M. their Beagle howled and howled and howled. It drove the neighbors nearly mad, kept small children from taking their naps, yet these dog owners could never understand the dog haters in their building. Fortunately, they moved.

A walk down any city street will reveal people with dogs on a leash who stand there and watch their animals soil the sidewalk. What could be more inconsiderate than that? There are people who own dogs and who will not teach them not to jump on people, and in some cases, not to bite or nip. People have dogs that chase cars and cause accidents, even human deaths. I have a friend who was thrown from his motor scooter and seriously injured when attacked by a dog. My son was thrown from his bicycle by someone else's very ill-mannered pooch. And how about the cat owner who allows his pet to wander over and booby-trap a neighbor's bird feeder? What does it all add up to? Good manners on the part of the pet and owner alike. You and your children are not the only ones who have to learn to live in this world. Your pet does, too, and your pet, like your children, reflects your intelligence and sensitivity.

What is a well-behaved dog? What are the constituents of good canine behavior? We may concede that our pets and our neighbor's pets should be well behaved, but how do we communicate and instill good behavior in pets? A dog has a limited capacity for commands. It can learn a certain number and no more, and although capacities may vary from dog to dog, there is a limit for every animal. Here is what I consider essential.

First, every dog should learn to come when he is called. Note, I say when he is called, not when he feels like it. One word is all that should be used, *come*. A dog should learn to sit the instant the command is given: again, a single-word command, *sit*. A dog should also learn to lie down on command of a hand signal or the word *down*. Please note, we don't say "sit down" or "come here" or "lie down." *Come, sit, down* will do and will not confuse. Another important one-word command is *no*. That means "stop whatever you are doing, immediately." *Stay* is a very important one. It means "stay where you are until I tell you to move."

A little trickier than the rest to convey, *heel* is also essential. It means the dog should move around to your left side and walk with his nose about on the level with your leg. It is the only sane way to walk a dog; no one looks sillier than when they are being dragged all over the lot by a panting, straining dog on a leash.

If all of this seems too much for an individual owner, there are very good books available that give details on how to get these commands across, and that also tell how to deal with problems. It is unlikely that your dog will come up with a new problem that hasn't been dealt with before—not just once but many times.

In many communities, there are very good obedience schools where owners can go one or two nights a week with their dog. Dog and master learn together, and that is probably the best way of all. It can be fun and many people who start out to get a few basic commands under control end up going on to obedience classes in dog shows.

Of course, in fun-and-games time, *fetch* is a must, and when the dog has brought the ball or stick, the command can be *drop* or *drop it*. If you really must shake hands with your dog, *paw* will do nicely (dogs seem to like to shake hands, paws, once they know how). Dogs are fun, they are a pleasure to have around, but they are never as much fun or as much pleasure as when they are well behaved. After all, even if you want to spoil your dog, *come, sit, down, no, stay, heel, fetch, drop* (or *drop it*), and *paw* aren't too much for him.

They won't cramp his style or crush his personality. Even in our time of permissiveness, those are not too much to ask in return for bed, board, and love.

Spaying Your Bitch: It seems that no matter how much is written about getting female dogs spayed, misinformation and confusion persists. Just for the record, here are the facts. An ovario-hysterectomy performed on a dog—the removal of her reproductive organs—is major surgery. It is performed under general anesthesia and there is an inevitable small element of risk. This is so very small, however, in light of the number of times it is performed every year, that risk should not be an excuse to postpone or decide against the operation.

The reasons for having it done are several and significant. It prevents the heat cycle, makes the bitch cleaner to have around, and does away with the problem of courting males carrying on in your front yard and generally making a nuisance of themselves. It does prevent accidental pregnancy and it does prevent diseases of the uterus that are fairly common in unspayed bitches. Spaying prevents false pregnancy, another fairly common annoying condition. Spaying also reduces the occurrence of breast tumors in dogs.

The most important consideration of all, however, is that spaying is the only really good means of birth control in dogs—it helps reduce the tragic production of unwanted puppies. Most veterinarians like to perform this surgery before the first heat, at six to seven months of age. Others prefer to wait until one heat has passed. You really have to pick your veterinarian and rely on him or her on all such questions.

Postoperative care for a spayed bitch is minimal, and most animals can go home after a day or two. There is trauma with general anesthesia, and it is a good idea to

let all of that pass before moving the animal very far.
A quiet day or so in the hospital is a wise precaution.
The stitches can come out anytime after the first week.
Some doctors prefer to wait ten days. Complications,
while certainly known, are uncommon.

Will spaying alter your pet's personality? No, except
it may reduce the desire to wander. Will spaying make
your pet fat and lazy? No, though an ill-considered
diet will. There is no valid reason for not spaying a pet,
other than the desire to have puppies. That is a major
decision and should not be considered unless the dog is
a super example of the breed and her puppies are
needed for the good of the breed.

Altering the Male Dog: Most intelligent people know
they should have female dogs spayed, but rather few
people realize that the males, too, should be neutered.
What does neutering mean in actual physical terms?
Well, your dog can have a vasectomy, but most people
feel castration is better. The surgery takes less than half
an hour. It is done under general anesthesia and is
painless. The small postoperative discomfort is too
slight to bother about. No great change takes place in
the altered male's personality—that is old wives' nonsense—but the dog is less likely to wander because the
scent of a female in heat will not have the same charms
for him. And because he will not wander as much, he
will be less likely to get into fights or to lose out in an
argument with a car or truck. Will he get fat? Not unless
you overfeed him. If his activity has been reduced because he is no longer a roamer (dogs should be kept at
home anyway), some small adjustment in his diet will
be called for.

So neutering can have a settling influence on your
pet, particularly if you live near people with an un-

spayed bitch. Does it do any good in the overall picture of pet overpopulation? Sure it does. It is true, of course, that bitches produce the puppies, but a bitch is only in heat twice a year, while a male can be sexually active twelve months of every year. A single male on the prowl can mate with a long succession of females. Both sexes should be neutered.

I think many people are slower to have surgery done on the male than on the female because so many men project and find the very concept of castration rough to live with. I am not being funny when I say that; I do believe it to be true. We live partly through the things we love, people and pets both. We should overcome our unconscious in this case. Male and female dogs alike are healthier, happier animals if they are neutral. And think of all the puppies that will not have to be killed. (Of course there is the exception of the outstanding example of the breed whose genetic potential is needed. That should be, though, the only exception.)

Dog Nutrition: There are three basic forms of dog food on the market today: the dry, which has been around for a long time; the canned, also an established idea; and the semimoist, which is only a few years old. Add to these the frozen horsemeat packets, and you have something like fifteen thousand different dog foods being marketed in the United States. Many varieties are local or regional, but a surprising number are national. Which is best?

The dried, especially when purchased in bulk sacks, is very much cheaper. Dry food is about ninety percent food, while canned dog food is only twenty-five percent food (that other seventy-five percent is water). That makes dry food more economical, but still, is it best? It is good enough for most kennels, most breeders, most veterinary hospitals, although everyone knows that animals are individuals and have to be treated in different ways. You feed that food which gives the best weight gain, best weight maintenance, which seems to please, and which gives healthy stools—just as you would with a child.

Dry food also has the advantage of being easier to use. No cans to open or dispose of, or to attract rats and insects, and no spooning or waste. If you practice self-feeding, leaving food for your dog to eat ad lib, it is a lot more practical and savory to leave a bowl of dry food around than canned meat, which will smell, attract insects, and harden into an unpalatable mass. Dry food has the advantage, too, of allowing your pet to use his teeth. That helps keep tartar under control and is good for gums.

Most dogs would probably select canned food over dried food because the smell is stronger, but once a dog is established on a dry-food diet, he will be happy on it. A lot of people moisten dry food with water or add table scraps, gravy, or vegetable water from the stove. For a large dog, you can put in an eighth to a half of a can of moist food. There are all kinds of ways to do it. It is a matter, certainly, to be discussed with your veterinarian. The most important thing is that your individual dog gets what he or she needs for its own long, healthy life.

First Aid for Dogs: How different are the first-aid directions for dealing with a dog from those followed when the victim is human? Not very, since both creatures are warm-blooded mammals.

There is one special consideration that we seldom encounter when dealing with a human accident victim, and that is the safety of the person administering first aid. It can be a problem with a dog, for even the best-behaved pet can be temporarily maddened by fear and pain and will bite. It is a good idea to gently but firmly muzzle a dog that has been injured. A necktie, a strip of cloth, any relatively wide, soft material can be used. The muzzle should not be tight enough to add to the animal's distress, but it should be firm enough to offer you real protection.

The two biggest killers in any accident, whether it involves man or animal, are bleeding and shock. The first and most obvious rule is *stop the bleeding*. Nothing you can do for a dog will mean very much if it bleeds to death. Pressure bandages usually work, but if an artery has been cut, you may have to use a tourniquet. Obviously, it is vital that the animal be placed in the hands of a veterinarian as soon as possible.

Dogs are very sensitive animals, and they react to whatever is going on around them. Keeping them quiet and holding the fuss down are good ideas. Cover the injured animal to conserve body heat—shock is second only to blood loss in importance. If the animal has been hit by a car or otherwise badly traumatized, there can be broken bones or internal injuries. Avoid moving the animal any more than is absolutely necessary. After it has been muzzled, slide it onto a board, blanket, anything that can be used as a stretcher. It may be wise to tie the animal onto a board if it has to be moved very far.

Do not give the animal water until a veterinarian has said it is all right to do so. If it is hyperventilating, its mouth can be moistened, but nothing should be given internally. Once you have checked for any bleeding, have secured the animal for transport to a hospital, and done what you can to keep it calm and minimize shock, you really have done all you can before the veterinarian takes over. Too much first aid is often counterproductive, because enthusiasm soon exceeds common sense. The best rule is, do as little as possible beyond stopping the bleeding and avoiding or ameliorating shock, and get the victim into the hands of a doctor—that goes equally for human and animal victims.

Dog Fleas: The scientific name of this little pest is *Ctenocephalides canis,* and his hind legs are longer than his front. That helps him push his way between the hairs of your poor dog.

Fleas are not all that particular. If a dog isn't handy, a cat will do, and failing that, a dog flea will take a ride on a person. They prefer babies, then youngsters, then women. Men come last in their order of preference. The dog flea has claws at the ends of its six feet, a spiny head comb, and leg bristles. The mouth is equipped with three hypodermiclike tubes that are used to pierce flesh and suck blood. The flea doesn't have a nose, but he doesn't need one, either. He breathes through vents in his body. The lady flea is the larger of the two.

These pesty little animals reproduce through copulation, and that can require up to nine hours. The female lays eggs not on the dog, but in cracks in the floor and other private places. Both fleas bring dried food to the egg-laying site (undigested dog blood) for the larvae to feed on. When the eggs hatch, anywhere from two to twelve days after being deposited, tiny thread-like worms emerge. After a week or so, they grow to be five millimeters long and then double up into a U-shape and spin their cocoons. Between one and two weeks later, an adult flea develops in the cocoon. When that adult will hatch out is anyone's guess. It can take a year, but when it does emerge, that flea is hungry and immediately starts looking for a meal. It will jump as high as eighteen inches and hang onto a bush, chair leg, or any other platform, waiting for a meal to come by. Happily, dog fleas do not commonly carry diseases from dog to man the way rat fleas can carry plague, but they certainly can make your dog's life miserable. If your dog is heavily infested, see your veterinarian and he will tell you of sprays and powders to use. Be sure to treat the baseboards of your house, around the edges of carpets, and other areas recommended on the spray can. The sprays will not kill eggs or the pupae of fleas, so treatments must be repeated at suggested intervals.

Worms: If you have a sandwich or other food in your hand, put it down for about two minutes. We are going to discuss worms in dogs, the second biggest parasite problem pet owners have (the first is fleas). Dogs can become infected with worms while still in their mother. Some worms can be passed on in the mother's milk, and puppies and grown dogs alike can pick up worms from infected food or dirt left by other dogs. Dogs do not get worms from eating sweets and starches. That is an old wives' tale.

There are three kinds of intestinal worms usually found in dogs. They are roundworm, hookworm, and tapeworm. The roundworm looks rather like a pale white earthworm and can grow to be seven inches long. It swims freely in the animal's intestine and lives off the food the dog takes in. A heavily infested dog loses coat luster, becomes listless, and sometimes bloated. Diarrhea is also a symptom of heavy infestation. Hookworms are much smaller, about three-quarters of an inch, and threadlike. They attach themselves to the dog's intestinal wall and suck blood. The coat will show infestation by losing its nice, healthy look, and the dog can become anemic and emaciated. The skin can become seriously scaly in fairly short order. The tapeworm is really a colony of independent segments, each about half an inch long. Inside the dog, the whole chain can be two feet long. An infected dog loses its healthy look and becomes colicky. There is diarrhea and the appetite fails.

It is easy for a veterinarian to tell if your dog has worms and which kind he has, if he has been infected. It is also easy for him to clean your dog out in very short order. He cannot, however, diagnose and treat an animal he has not seen. Do not wait for symptoms to show up; have your dog checked regularly by your veterinarian, and keep him happy and healthy all his life long. One hint to save yourself and your veterinarian time and trouble: when you take your dog in, take a stool sample along. It is necessary for microscopic examination. Now you can go back to that sandwich.

Canine Heartworm: As man becomes more mobile, so do his problems—in our own bodies and in and on the bodies of our domestic animals and plants, we spread disease and parasites. Problems that were once restricted geographically know no boundaries now, for they too can ride a 747 and sail in a ship. One such problem is canine heartworm. As our dogs have been shipped around—for shows, field trials, hunting trips—and as we have changed our addresses, this potentially fatal parasite has spread. It is a growing problem.

First, some facts. Canine heartworm cannot be passed to a human being. There is no danger from that. Some other animals can get it, apparently, but *not* human beings. Neither do dogs pass it on to each other directly. There must be an intermediary host, a mosquito. When one sucks a dog's blood, its gets microscopic versions of the worm. Once inside the mosquito, the worm begins to grow and develop; within two or three weeks the mosquito is ready to infect another dog —it feeds and passes the parasite along. Once in the dog, the worm seeks the right side of the heart and the adjacent blood vessels, and can grow to be two feet long.

Eventually, the worms migrate into the dog's lungs, and the infestation can prove fatal. It need not, however, for your veterinarian has medicines to prevent this disease, even to cure it. Watch for a change in temperament, a general loss of tone, listen for excessive coughing. Heartworm is a worse problem where the mosquito season runs long. Mosquitoes have a season of sorts everywhere in the United States, and the problem can be judged national. Remember these key facts: your veterinarian can prevent it in your dog, he can cure it in your dog, and you are in no danger at all. Knowing those facts can take the terror out of this widely publicized problem.

Distemper: What is distemper, besides one of the most dreaded words in dogdom? There seems to be a lot of confusion and not just a little misinformation on the subject.

Distemper is a very highly contagious virus disease of dogs. The symptoms are high temperature, gastrointestinal and respiratory distress, and sometimes lung and neurological complications. It is a killer, especially of young animals, although it is by no means limited to puppies. The virus that causes distemper is always present where dogs are found and puppies are exposed very early in life. In the first days of life, the pup is protected by natural immunity that comes to it through its mother's milk. After that, it needs your help.

The disease distemper is transmitted through contaminated objects and by what is known as the aerosol-droplet route; that is, it can be airborne. The incubation period usually runs six to nine days. The first symptom of distemper is fever, and that can persist for one to three days with no other signs. It then drops back down to normal for a day or two before shooting up again. This second fever bout can last a week or even more. The eyes become inflamed and begin to discharge, there can be a nasal discharge, and the animal will tend to squint against bright light. Diarrhea and general depression set in, and coughing can mark the onset of a potentially fatal pneumonia.

Even if the dog survives these first worrisome symptoms, there can be fatal neurological complications, such as convulsions, aimless wandering, and disorientation. The disease may be mild in one dog and violent in another. There may be periods of apparent recovery with increasingly more violent relapses. The whole course can be run in ten days to two weeks, or can hang on for weeks or even months.

None of this need occur, however, and almost all pups can be successfully immunized so that when the immunity imparted by the mother wears off, other protection will take over. When the puppy should be immunized depends on several determinations that only a veterinarian can make. Whether your pup should be bridged over to the four-month plateau with a shot that can be given as early as three weeks depends on a number of factors. But there is absolutely no question that protection is essential and is available.

The first stop with any new puppy, no matter where you get it, should be a veterinarian. You should have in your hand for his examination a full statement of all shots given up to the moment of your taking possession of your new family member. Not all cases of distemper are the result of owner carelessness, but most of them are.

Rabies: The word rabies so strikes terror into the hearts of people that it is a good idea to check the facts. We still have rabies in this country, although incidence is far below former levels. It will be very hard to eradicate rabies altogether as long as we are contiguous to Mexico, where it is a really serious problem. How are things going here?

There has not been a case of human rabies transmitted in an urban area of the United States since 1963. The last case of dog rabies in Philadelphia was in 1948, but the area is not entirely clear, since a case of fox rabies was identified in 1971. There has not been a case of human rabies acquired from a pet in New York City since 1944, and no case of rabies in dogs has been identified in the city since 1955. Dogs no longer need be held in New York after a bite accident unless there is reason to suspect that the dog might have the disease. Dog bites are still reportable in the city, however, where over forty thousand occur each year.

There is, then, no need for panic in the event of a dog bite, but the animal should be seen by a veterinarian and should be watched very carefully for at least ten days to be certain there are no behavioral changes. Any bite from a wild animal—fox, skunk, bat, squirrel, rat; any mammal, really—should be evaluated by health authorities. There is a big difference between panic and reasonable precaution. Any parent whose child is bitten and who fails to contact the appropriate health authorities and see a doctor is, or at least could be, playing with that child's life, for animals are as mobile as people and move with their human families. Dogs moving into an area where rabies is all but unknown could reverse the situation overnight, and indeed that has happened.

Because of hard work by health authorities, responsible behavior by pet owners who have had their animals inoculated, and perhaps even a little good luck, rabies is far down in this country—down but not gone, so get rabies shots for your pets.

As for recognizing the symptoms: look for unnatural reactions to sound and light in a dog, and watch for any sign of facial paralysis or difficulty in walking. A drunken, tottering walk could mean trouble. The term *hydrophobia* refers, in the case of rabies, to a kind of paralysis that makes it impossible for a dog to drink, so that it appears to fear water. A dog with rabies is a very sick animal, and its owner should be able to see immediately that something is desperately wrong.

One day we will have universal laws that require every dog to have rabies shots. They are not expensive, they are safe, and not particularly painful. Until such laws exist, it is up to the individual pet owner to take the necessary, responsible steps.

Dog Bite: Nearly forty thousand people were bitten by dogs in New York City in 1975, and it is estimated that nationally, over fifty million dollars a year is spent on medical bills repairing and caring for dog-bite victims. What should you know about dog bite?

Not all dog bites are avoidable by the victim. Some are, perhaps a great many are—we do not have figures. There are some things you can teach your children and perhaps keep in mind for yourself. First, most dogs won't bite you. They are more apt to lick you. Dogs, by nature for most breeds, like people. That is how they have been bred for somewhere between ten and twenty thousand years. Still, even the best dog can have a bad day. Don't teach your children to be afraid of dogs, just careful with them, as they are with cars and trucks, tools, and stairways.

If you are approaching a dog to pat it, don't bring

your hand down on top of its head. That can be misinterpreted as a threatening motion. Slowly bring your hand up in front and under the dog's nose so that it can see and smell it and not be frightened by it. It is generally best not to hug or attempt to pick up a strange dog. If the dog is attended, ask the owner's permission before approaching or touching it. It may or may not like strangers. Some breeds love their families, but are suspicious of people they don't know. Children running and screaming past a dog can trigger that dog into chasing and biting. Walk by a strange, unattended dog, perhaps saying something nice and soothing to it. If a dog sounds threatening, move away from it slowly; don't bolt and run. You probably couldn't outrun it anyway.

Many dogs are very protective of their owners and will bite if they think their owners are being attacked. When someone you know is with his or her dog, don't dash up and grab him, hug him, or do anything that could appear to be an attack without asking about his dog.

In general, leave unattended dogs alone, and ask the right questions before becoming involved with an attended one. Teach your kids to ask permission before putting their hands out. If you have to help an animal in trouble, one hit by a car, for example, use a necktie to muzzle it before you attempt to lift it. Picking up a frightened dog in pain is one good way of getting bitten in the face or neck. Dogs are our friends, they have been for a long time, but bites occur, and certainly it is possible to prevent at least some of them.

The Vicious Dog: There is no excuse for it. You have no right to own a vicious dog. It is a matter of simple responsibility. The potential damage a vicious dog, especially a large vicious dog, can do to a human being is hideous. I have seen bite cases, bad bite cases where the injuries are permanently disfiguring even after extensive plastic surgery. Nothing you may think about your own life-style justifies your forcing this measure of risk on other people in your community. You simply have no right to own a vicious dog.

We could talk for hours about what makes a dog vicious. I would wager that in most cases it is human contact, the way the dog was taught to respond to people. There may be naturally bad dogs; in fact, I know there are. I once had one. Out of about twenty-five dogs I have owned, one bad one. More usually, dogs are made vicious purposely or inadvertently by man. If you have a biter or snapper or especially an attacker, I would see a professional trainer right away. The habit must be broken permanently. If it can't be, the trainer will tell you, then the dog should go. It isn't easy to get rid of a dog. I have had to do it. I guess I love the fool creatures as much as any man alive—we have six at the moment—but there are times when your responsibility to your fellow man must override your own tastes and loves and sensitivities. You can't go driving through school zones at seventy miles an hour, you can't have rifle practice in your backyard in the suburbs, you can't buzz residences with your private plane, and you can't keep a dog that is vicious. You don't need a vicious dog for a watchdog—that requires barking, not ripping out the jugular vein.

Remember, a vicious dog, however he got that way and however good a pet he might have been if things had worked out differently for him, is a loaded gun, ready to go off. Worse, perhaps, for with the vicious dog, you don't have control of the trigger. Think about it if you have such a dog, before you find yourself with a hospital emergency case and a court case, too.

Stock Killers: What do you do when a dog you love goes sour, at least in a social sense? I have friends and they have a lovely Sporting Dog. Not very long ago, I dined with these friends and spent some happy time with their very pleasant and very handsome animal. Then, two days later, the storm broke. Because my friends live on a fair parcel of land, they let their dog out free, but the dog found a neighbor who had something irresistible to offer—livestock. In minutes, five laying hens were dead and one prize rooster was madder than a hornet, with no tail feathers left at all. Next came the sheep, but all my friends' dog had time to do was stampede them before he was spotted and shouted at, and then he took off.

Where does responsibility lie? Does the farmer have the right to kill that dog the next time he catches him at his stock? Morally I think he does, after fair warning to the owners, although I certainly can't speak for local laws and local custom. Clearly the responsibility is with the owners. The dog will have to be restrained. No one has the right to loose a dog that is a threat to the life or property of other people. It is going to be hard on my friends, because their dog is not going to react well to restraint after all his freedom. He will be noisy about it and perhaps even sullen, and he will work on ways to escape. But, if they don't solve the problem, they had better give the dog away.

Anyone giving a dog away that is a stock killer is obligated to tell prospective owners of this very bad fault. You cannot duck it. If your pet has been killing livestock around you, or just running it, he will do the same elsewhere unless steps are taken to prevent it.

Running, by the way, is no joke for the farmer. In beef cattle it means weight loss, and in dairy cattle it means reduced milk production. You can, of course, get a professional dog trainer in to work on the problem.

It is sometimes correctable, but until the problem is solved, your dog, once he develops this bad habit, has to be tied up very carefully. Bad habits in dogs are not permissible, certainly not when they infringe on the rights of other people.

The Feral Dog: They run deer to death. They raise havoc with smaller mammals, reptiles and amphibians, and ground-nesting birds. I speak of a scourge, the feral dog.

Feral, in the sense we are using it here, means anything that was once domestic that has returned to the wild. There are feral trees, mustangs are feral horses, and, unfortunately, there are feral dogs. No one, and that means no one, knows how much damage they do, but at least one conservation magazine has seen fit to call them the hounds of hell. Arkansas is engaged in a research project to determine the exact role of the feral dog in the wildlife picture. My guess is they won't be happy with what they find. Preliminary reports from other states suggest the feral dog's role is a harsh one.

A free-running dog probably has a life span of under two years, and a dog doesn't have to be two years old to breed and create more feral dogs. Who is to blame for this disastrous situation? We are. The city dweller who rents a summer cottage and picks up a puppy from the pound for the kids to play with and then abandons it; he is certainly to blame. (And his kind numbers in the tens of thousands, believe it or not.) The person who owns a dog that he does not intend to breed as a serious endeavor and fails to get his bitch spayed; he is as guilty as anyone.

In the next couple of years, we will see what these kinds of people have wrought. We already know these dogs are a potential reservoir for rabies; they attack people (children have been killed in some cases); they are listed in a number of states as the only serious predator on livestock within that state; and they do cross with coyotes to produce wily coydogs. All this because some people simply will not do their part, will not take the steps they know in their hearts, such as they are, they should take. All America is paying the bill—over $200 million a year to collect and destroy unwanted feral dogs and cats. They are born at the rate of thousands an hour, every day and night of the year.

No Dogs Allowed—In Some Places: In summer, a lot of people hit the holiday road and some take their pets along. They can be disgruntled to find that dogs, at least, are not welcome in many places. Lest we dog owners get paranoid about it, it is not a bad idea to review some of the reasons why this is often so. Usually, but not always, the *no-dog* rule is the result of bad manners on the part of previous dog owners. Beaches, very often, are closed to dogs. Why? Because other owners didn't clean up when their dog made a mess, and who wants their kid rolling around in that! Or perhaps they had dogs that tended to be snappy and failed to keep them under control. Lots of dog-bite cases occur on summer beaches. So obey the no-dogs-on-the-beach rule where it is posted, and if you are allowed on with your pet, control it and clean up after it, or you may come back another time and find no dogs allowed.

Zoos generally do not want dogs on the premises because, quite frankly, they do not feel that all pet owners are as good to their animals as the zoos are to theirs. They are afraid of disease and, also, of people who will not control their animals, which can mean harassment of the zoo animals and dog bites for other visitors. Wildlife refuges don't want pets, very often, because pets get lost and are hazardous to the animals being preserved by reason, once again, of disease and harassment. In parks, dogs can be a nuisance because they get lost, they stir up local wildlife, they carry disease, and they bite other visitors. You see, the theme is repeated over and over again.

What is the lesson? Well, from one dog owner to another, I would say there are just too many people in our ranks who have bad manners and think they have some kind of heaven-decreed right to do as they will. Lest non–dog owners pick up on that and try to make something of it that isn't there, I would point out that automobile owners with bad manners contribute to our staggering fifty-five thousand highway deaths a year, and hi-fi owners with bad manners ruin a lot of people's sleep, not to mention their hearing. It all boils down to people being considerate of others. The pets, in this case, are almost incidental.

Dogs in Cars: My wife and I once took my son's dog to a large dog show in New Jersey. My son was working and couldn't be there himself. It was a blistering hot day, well up in the nineties, and this was a big show. Trailers and campers from as far away as California were in the lot. People had arrived early and set up tents and shelters. Many were lounging under them between classes, some with coolers for their beer and sandwiches. The line at the refreshment stand was long, and the local fire department auxiliary was selling iced tea and hamburgers at inflated prices. Superb dogs were being moved back and forth, others were being groomed. The attentive owners had their dogs wrapped or draped in damp towels. It was so hot one English Bulldog fainted and had to be given oxygen.

Despite the terrible heat, the loudspeaker kept pleading with owners to check their cars for dogs in distress. *Eleven times* by actual count in one two-hour period! Some so-called fanciers had locked their dogs in the cars in the blazing sun. "There is a car with Rhode Island plates," the speaker blared, "with two Borzois in it. The police report the dogs appear to be in deep distress. Please check your car." Again and again and again we heard such announcements. Each time an angry murmur would roll through the crowd, and it was clear most of the people there were dog lovers. One young exhibitor announced that he had heard enough. He headed for the parking lot announcing he was going to smash every window in any car with a dog in it. I don't know how far he went with his plan.

It should hardly be necessary to remind people that dogs are living, feeling creatures. They are not packages that can be checked and picked up "sometime." If they are taken along, they have to be taken into account, whether that is to a dog show, on a shopping trip, or along on vacation. If a dog is too much trouble, determine that beforehand, for once you do take your dog, you are obligated to see to its welfare no matter how your plans develop. After all, if the dog *is* along, it was your idea, you extended the invitation.

Dog Shows: I get a lot of questions about dog shows, and there is the persistent misconception that the show world of purebred dogs is strictly for the very rich and the very much at leisure. That is simply not true, and I fear it keeps some people from participating in a sport they would love. First, showing one or more dogs is a family activity, and when you walk among the grooming stands and along the ringsides at a show today, you see family groups—adults, kids, friends, and grandparents, all there watching for the big moment—and when a favorite pet is picked, there are tears, not just a little shouting, and a whole big bunch of happiness.

Once upon a time, the dog show was strictly an elitist affair, and the rich participated from afar with handlers and groomers and kennel masters doing all the work and calling in the results that might be toasted in fine Madeira a thousand miles away. There is still some of that, of course, but that is no longer what it is all about. Policemen, firemen, insurance salesmen, salesgirls, secretaries, and social workers, they are all into it, and the world of the purebred dog is the better for it. Junior showmanship is big now, too—teenagers being judged on their skills in obtaining and maintaining condition in a dog, and on their skill at presenting it in the ring. The kids doing it are poised, and they earn their rewards by hard work. There has been some criticism of some exceptionally wealthy owners turning top show dogs over to their kids to take into junior showmanship and dazzle the judge away from his real task, to judge the progress of the youngsters. There is some of that, but junior showmanship is still a great activity.

A lot of people are confused, I think, about the way a dog show works. It really isn't very complicated. In each of the 123 breeds, there are preliminary classes. The winners of each of these classes compete until judging boils down to one male and one female, a winner's dog and a winner's bitch. Those two go against each other and against any champion dogs that have been entered. Champions, dogs and bitches who have already won fifteen points, don't have to enter the preliminary classes. The winning dog and winning bitch and the established champions in the breed (known as specials) compete for the familiar best-of-breed title. Then all of the best-of-breed dogs within each group compete, all the Toys, all the Terriers, all the Sporting Dogs, Working Dogs, Hounds, and Non-Sporting Dogs.

The animals are not competing against each other, but against their respective breed standards. The judge determines which dog in the ring comes closest to perfection according to its own standard. There are six best-in-groups, then, and from them at the end of the show is selected the best-in-show.

A dog that can go as far as group judging and take a group win is a splendid example of the breed, and what this all does, besides giving a lot of people pleasure and some people profit, is elevate the standard of the breed and keep it high. The new, young dogs that take the preliminary classes must battle against the established perfection of older, more experienced dogs for that difficult best-of-breed title.

Judging in a dog show is a touchy subject. A great many people now show dogs as a hobby, and a question often asked is, Are dog-show judges fair and honest? Some people have heard me report on how horse shows are very often fixed or rigged, and they want to know if the same is true of dog shows. I do not believe so. I have seen too many fine, conscientious, and really knowledgeable judges take too long going over each animal and then giving the prize to what was obviously the best animal in the class or competition. I have also seen, as has everyone who has been to dog shows, a judge who either did not know the breed or didn't care about the animals at all. Barely looking at the dogs except to put on just enough show to get away with it, he then passed out the ribbons to handler friends. Undeniably, there are judges who pin friends, not dogs, and they are known to the show-dog world as political hacks and not true judges at all. It is quite typical for people showing their dogs to call each other up and say, "Forget such-and-such a show. Bozo Bigfoot is judging the Hounds. . . ." or ". . . Gertie Green-gums is judging Toys." People just bypass the show. We have. In time, one hopes, these hacks will be driven out, although there will probably always be a few around. They are in every field.

I would say, though, that the vast majority of dog-show judges are honest, devoted experts who have spent a lifetime working toward the perfection of the finest in purebred companion animals. They want fine, young dogs to make a showing, and they want established leaders of the breed to continue being awarded high and coveted awards. It is when breeders work like the devil to defeat an established best-in-show dog that they turn out the best dogs they possibly can. Some people wonder why, when a dog like Gold Rush Charlie, the all-time top-winning Golden Retriever in history, wins his thirty-fifth best-in-show, they keep on showing him. It is because he is the standard of perfection that another Golden Retriever will have to match or surpass, and it is in striving for that goal that breeders do their most for the breed. Yes, I think more than enough of the dog-show judges working today are better than honest; they are devoted. As for the hacks that pin their handler friends and not the best dogs, just sneer at them. They will go the way of all hacks, and we won't even go to their funerals.

Dog shows are big business, of course, but they are also a hobby for thousands and thousands of people. Even a moderate-sized show may have between one thousand and fifteen hundred dogs entered, and it does give dogdom its glamor and a lot of excitement.

Raising, showing, and taking great pride in a pet is an activity for a family that is all pulled together. It is just one more way animals work within our life-style to make things just a little bit better. Happily, it is some-

thing just about any family can do, and if showing isn't
right for you, go as a spectator. Why *not* go to a dog
show near where you live and spend a day seeing how
it happens?

Andrew: I would like to pay tribute to a small life. His
name was Andrew. His total life span was about eight
weeks. My wife and daughter found him in a dreadful
pound they were helping inspect. He was about five
weeks old and very small. He had been thrown in with
about twenty other dogs, mostly adults. There were two
full-grown German Shepherds fighting, and Andrew,
all two and a quarter pounds of him, cowered in the
corner. In the middle of the melee was a pan of hard,
unmoistened kibble, food Andrew couldn't possibly
handle, yet he was supposed to fight for it or die. Anyway, Andrew came home to be our sixth dog, emaciated, sickly, undersized, bones protruding. What a start
in life.

First there was diarrhea, and it took days to bring it
under control. He was infested with two species of
worms. They had to be seen to as well. Then, predict-
ably, despite the fact that he had been given shots
within two hours of my daughter's claiming him, he
came down with distemper. The diarrhea started up
again, he wouldn't or couldn't eat. There was the
coughing and the choking and the temperature. The
difference between life and death for a dog that young
is nursing care, so my mother-in-law, my wife, and my
daughter took turns feeding him with an eyedropper
every two hours, night and day. It was a heroic battle
to help Andrew in his fight to stay alive. He was bright,
he was alert for a time, and then he would sink again.
Finally he broke through; the temperature went, the
appetite returned, all the good signs. He had rickets,

that was obvious, he had had a bad start, but he wanted to live. Then, just when it seemed certain that little Andrew would make it—he was up to two and three-quarters pounds—there was an unaccountable accident. He was in a room with several large dogs, all good dogs, but perhaps he tried to take one's food. Something like that. There was a momentary show of temper and a snap, perhaps intended as a warning, and Andrew's jaw was broken. Our veterinarian tried, but Andrew's start in life had been too rough. He had had too little food at the beginning, and the bone would not knit. Nor was it large enough to pin. While Andrew was still under the anesthesia where he had been placed for X-raying, the decision was made. His sleep would go deeper, and he would suffer no more.

Why, we must ask, was Andrew born? Why was that bitch, that unnamed, random-bred bitch, allowed to breed and produce yet another waif? We already have millions of them waiting to die. Here's to Andrew, and curses be to that person who allowed him to be born.

3

THE DOG BREEDS

THE SPORTING BREEDS

Irish Setter: The breed was already two centuries old in the British Isles when first known in this country, just after the agony of the Civil War.

Although the Irish Setter goes back to the late seventeenth century, it wasn't until the early 1800s that the red Irish Setter evolved in Ireland. Up until that time, he had been a red-and-white dog of uncertain origin. Some say he is down from that strange-looking dog, the Irish Water Spaniel, crossed with the Irish Terrier, and others hold that a combination of English Setter, Spaniel, Pointer, and Gordon Setter gave us this handsome red dog. We will never know. Those kinds of records just don't crop up anymore.

The red Setter stands to twenty-six inches at the shoulder, and the male can weigh up to sixty pounds. The coat is flat and of moderate length, its color golden-red chestnut or tending toward mahogany. No white or black is allowed now. This Setter, like all Setters, was originally a hunting dog, and he was apparently without peer. But he was so handsome that breeders on this side of the Atlantic saw him as a decorative pet and began breeding for that. Although he is still a country rather than a city dog, he is usually a pet today and is seldom used for hunting.

The Irish Setter is probably the most temperamental of all the Setters, perhaps of all the Sporting Dogs. He is high-strung and requires a great deal of training if he is not to be a first-rate clown and nuisance. He is headstrong and willful and lovable. He is also exceedingly affectionate and loyal, and not necessarily to just one person. He loves his family and may be either demonstrative or aloof with strangers—that varies. Irish Setters can be thieves, even stock killers, and they do wander, all of this when they are not properly trained. A breed I personally like very much, Irish Setters should belong only to strong people who truly love dogs and who are prepared to work with their charges and train them well.

Cocker Spaniel: Some years ago a Cocker Spaniel named My Own Brucie swept to victory at Madison Square Garden and caught the imagination of the public. The breed went on to almost unbelievable popularity. As an unfortunate consequence, a lot of breeders chose to bury their scruples and began to cash in. They all but ruined a marvelous Sporting breed. It is now making a comeback.

The American Cocker is known simply as the Cocker Spaniel, as opposed to its sister breed known as the English Cocker Spaniel. The standards call for the American Cocker to be fifteen inches tall; the English Cocker goes about two inches higher in the withers. Both animals are extremely elegant in appearance and movement and should be proud and gay.

In 1975 the Cocker was seventh in popularity in this country while the English Cocker was sixty-fifth. No one should even think of owning a Cocker Spaniel unless he really likes to care for a dog. Those marvelous long, feathered ears, that feathered chest, and those frills on the legs, all of that grand styling means combing and brushing and caring. It doesn't happen by itself.

The Cocker Spaniel is derived from old Spanish Sporting Dogs (hence the name Spaniel), and it does require exercise. Many examples have been bred down in their demands to make them better apartment dogs, but a Cocker that knows what the wind and grass are like is a better, happier dog, and his owner is a prouder and more satisfied person. The real quality of these super little field animals will return when they are again allowed to move with freedom in the world they were meant to inhabit.

Anyone seriously thinking of the breed now should be more than careful to consult the best specialty breeders in his or her area (beyond, if necessary) and buy only a dog whose parents are available for examination. A Cocker Spaniel with field-trail experience as well as bench-show ribbons is likely to be a better all-around dog. Silly, overbred mannequins can be snappy and unpleasant. The Cocker's nature was meant to be pleasant indeed, and nothing less should be acceptable to the new owner. There are still plenty of fine bloodlines around, and one day these will allow the Cocker Spaniel—the American version of the English adaptation of the Spanish Spaniel/Setter line—to return to former glory. In the meanwhile, take your time and buy only the best.

Labrador Retriever: We all like to deal in superlatives. We like to know which is the biggest, the best, the oldest, the richest. For those who would ask what is the best breed of dog in the world, we do not have an answer, but we do have a candidate, one of the finest of all, the Labrador Retriever.

The Lab does not come from Labrador. He is a product of Newfoundland. Toward the end of the eighteenth century, English fishermen working the Canadian coast picked up some Newfoundland dogs and brought them back to England, there they were crossed with various Retrievers, flat-coated and curly-coated kinds both. The result was the so-called Labrador Retriever we know and love today.

Another misconception: people speak of "Golden Labradors," and that leads to confusion with the true Golden Retriever, a different but equally sublime animal. The Lab is either black (he can be dark, dark brown) or yellow. So he is properly spoken of as a yellow Lab, not a golden.

The dog can run a little over two feet at the shoulder and weigh over seventy-five pounds. This is a solidly built animal. The coat is dense and short, shorter than the Golden's, and should not be wavy. The Lab is a hard-working dog, with more sense than a lot of people I have known. He is very even-tempered, calm, polite, gentle, and loyal beyond belief. He loves to work and he loves to play. Although he is reserved with strangers, he is never mean unless seriously mistreated. With kids he is ideal. He is usually smarter than they are and will watch over them. He will fetch a stick on land or from water for hours on end, and he will feel very sorry for himself if you don't let him carry things from time to time. It is kind just to let him carry your paper or a small bundle. It makes him feel needed and loved.

It would be foolish to say that the Labrador is the finest of all dogs (especially since we own a Golden), but certainly few, if any, dogs are brighter, more pleasant to have around, more reliable, faithful, and gentlemanly. They are strong and hardy and can stand any weather. They do need a lot of exercise and should be given a chance to run, preferably to retrieve, every day, no matter what the weather. They were born to work, and it is so built in that you can see the frustration in their behavior when they are not allowed to perform. I do not see them in an apartment.

Buy a Labrador Retriever from a professional breeder,

never from a pet shop, and watch out for hip dysplasia, a congenital deformity.

Golden Retriever: No question about it, the splendid Golden Retriever is one of the all-time great dogs: sensible, even-tempered, pleasant to the point of being charming. Not a fighter, he is happy to work, happy to play, happy just to be cared for and appreciated. He is a great hunting dog, one of the greatest ever, and a splendid pet. He is smart, alert, willing, and a lovely rich golden color. He weighs up to seventy-five pounds and stands two feet at the shoulder.

There are several theories as to where this incredible breed of dog came from, but this much seems certain: the place was England, and the ancestry probably Gordon Setter and Newfoundland Shepherd, with such issue crossed with a dog unknown to us today, the Tweed Water Spaniel. Stories about Russian circus dogs working into the line are probably closer to legend, but then, this is a dog that inspires legendry.

The question inevitably arises, should this dog be owned by city dwellers? I personally do not like to see large hunting dogs in cramped apartments, but if there ever was a breed that could make it anywhere, it is this one. Still, no one should dream of owning a Golden Retriever unless he is going to give it or allow it at least two hours of exercise a day . . . and that means really moving around. Weather means nothing to this breed— they will swim in freezing water with as much pleasure as they will later curl up in front of a fire. If you want a Golden and live in an urban area, take a vow that no matter what the weather and what your mood, you and your dog will be outdoors two of every twenty-four hours (and that is a *minimum*), and will keep on the move. It will be good for you, too.

The Golden is a perfect dog with children. All Goldens love all children, even when they get to playing roughhouse style. It is hard to imagine what an ill-tempered Golden Retriever would be like, they are such gloriously gentle animals.

Never buy a Golden from anyone but a specialty breeder. Unscrupulous mass-production breeders are shipping these dogs to pet shops by the crateload, and their careless breeding has spread the incidence of hip dysplasia, to which the Golden is particularly susceptible. Only a breeder who loves this breed above all others should have the privilege of selling one to you.

Brittany Spaniel: Early in the fifth century, warlike Irish chieftains crossed the English Channel and invaded Gaul, now France. They left many fragments of a strange heritage before returning to their homeland, and one of them may have been canine: their red-and-white Setter-like dogs, precursors of the Irish Setter, descendants of the hunting dogs of Spain. These Spanish-cum-Irish field dogs were bred to local French dogs, and from them may have come the ancestor of today's Brittany Spaniel.

That the Brittany is called a Spaniel at all is probably a trick of language. The male is over twenty inches tall and weighs to forty pounds. It is really a Setter, but then Setters and Spaniels are just animals bred up and down in size from a common ancestor. The Brittany does have a stub tail, as is true of Spaniels, but that is a characteristic only about a century old (as a matter of heredity from birth; their tails are not docked). The Brittany is orange and white, or liver and white, and the coat is dense, as is to be expected of a field dog. It is flat or wavy, not curly or silky, and is slightly on the coarse side as Spaniels go.

The Brittany Spaniel is a field dog, a Sporting Dog, and he belongs out of doors. He is fearless and aggressive. He makes a good watchdog—better than that, he makes a super water dog. He does tend to be one-mannish, very much so.

He is a very hard-nosed canine character and can be uncomfortable around strangers. And it is a sad fact that strangers are often uncomfortable around him, for he can be a serious biter. He just likes his own folks and nobody else—at least that is the characteristic of the breed. Of course, there are, as always, exceptions.

The Brittany is not a handsome dog as Spaniels and Setters go, but he is a superb field dog and will take endless training from a really authoritative trainer. A special dog, good for special people.

Springer Spaniel: His history may be traceable to the period before Christ, on the Iberian Peninsula, but these days we think of England and of Wales when we hear the name Springer Spaniel. We also think of quality.

There are two Springer Spaniels listed today among the Sporting breeds, the English Springer and the Welsh. An examination of four-hundred-year-old manuscripts and prints from Wales shows the dog there in approximately his present form, but the breed goes back much further than that. Exactly when it emerged we cannot say, but the Spaniel form (the Springer is a Land Spaniel as opposed to a Water Spaniel) may go back three thousand years in Spain. At least the dogs that apparently lived on the Iberian Peninsula that long ago were very Spaniel-like.

By 1387 A.D., a French nobleman who was addicted to the hunt wrote about the Spaniel as we know him now. We don't know when the dog arrived in England, or when he then drifted toward the north and west, but we do know that more than four centuries ago he was in Wales and Scotland developing into separate breeds. Today we have the English Springer—a dog eighteen to twenty inches tall and weighing up to fifty-five pounds—and the Welsh Springer—a dog sixteen to seventeen inches tall and weighing no more than forty pounds. There are slight differences in the coats of the two breeds. The English Springer has a medium-length coat that can be either flat or wavy, while the sporting Welshman has a straight or flat coat that is thick and silky. The coat should never be wiry or curly in either breed. More variety in color is allowed in the English breed. The Welsh Springer is always dark red and white; it is a rich-looking coat. The Englishman can have black, liver, white, tan, blue, a whole slew of colors and combinations.

Both breeds are smart, really smart. They are hunters, of course, land hunters, and when they are well bred and well trained, they can outshine almost any competition you put up against them. They are calm dogs, good with kids. They are, in fact, a combination of fine hunting dog, fine family dog, and reliable watchdog. They do need exercise, that is categorical. These are field dogs, and you shouldn't own one unless you are going to get it out where it can run, sniff, and learn to obey. You don't have to be a hunter, but simply someone who likes the combination of fresh air and smart dog. You should also not mind using a brush, or else your Springer will be a mess. The Welsh Springer, because he is considerably smaller than his English counterpart, may be favored for apartment life.

German Shorthaired Pointer: It can be fascinating to study dog origins and see how breeders of old constructed the dogs we know today.

For centuries, there was a Pointer in Spain that was neither particularly elegant nor very bright, but it had other qualities. In the 1600s, some of these Pointers were imported to Germany and crossed with native Bird Dogs. The nose of this new breed proved weak, however, and dogs that had been in France since the Crusades—Bloodhounds or Bloodhound-type dogs—were crossed in to improve scenting ability. That also made for heavier bones. The Germans next crossed in Terrier blood, from something like our modern Fox Terrier, which made the bones finer and increased speed, but this, in turn, made the dog lose its pointing instinct. So the breeders then imported the fine and very elegant Pointer from England, the dog we know today simply as the Pointer, and this gave their animal back its pointing abilities while retaining its very good nose and its aggressiveness with game. It also greatly improved its looks. We call that dog today the German Shorthaired Pointer.

This is a regal liver-and-white animal, either spotted or patched, that stands to twenty-five inches and weighs up to seventy pounds. He can be a first-rate family dog, but he needs enormous amounts of exercise. The German Shorthair is not for the apartment, and even the suburbs are questionable unless the dog is going to be exercised on a regular schedule. This is still a field dog, though he makes a great and affectionate pet and a very good watchdog. Like all of the European Shorthaired Pointer—like dogs, he is headstrong and even a little wild unless a firm hand is at the other end of the lead. This dog needs a master who knows what he is doing or is willing to take the dog to obedience school. When the German Shorthaired Pointer is fully under control, he is a lovely animal, as handsome as any you can get. He needs almost no grooming and is great in any weather: a Sporting Dog of top quality and with pet qualities to match.

Weimaraner: In Germany there is a field dog known as the red Schweisshund, a breed that must have come down in some way from the Bloodhound. From both of these breeds has come the dog we know as the Weimaraner. Twenty-seven inches tall, eighty-five pounds, mouse gray with a short, sleek coat, tail docked, and head high, this is some dog!

The Weimaraner was one of Germany's most jealously guarded animal resources. You couldn't get an example of the breed unless you were first accepted as member of a club, and you had to agree to all kinds of rules for breeding and registration. You even had to agree to kill poor examples born in your litters. Eventually, this control was cracked, and by 1929, the first animals were brought to America. In 1943 AKC recognition was accorded.

The Weimaraner is a hunting dog, but not one for a kennel. He is too gregarious; he belongs in the family, with his people. He is a better watchdog than are most hunting dogs, because he is aggressive and assertive. He is fine with children and a good all-around family dog. He needs and deserves a great deal of exercise and is a questionable choice for the city apartment, unless you spend a lot of time in the country as well or unless you like long, fast walks a couple of times a day. The Weimaraner can be the best-mannered dog in the world or the biggest pain in the you-know-what. It depends not so much on the dog as on the owner. These assertive, powerful, headstrong, extremely intelligent animals require an equally assertive, at least as intelligent, master or mistress. They want to be shown their guidelines, and if the training starts early and is consistent and persistent, then the Weimaraner is as fine an animal as there can be. But woe be to the weak or irresolute owner who sluffs off such responsibilities and hopes simply to keep this animal inside the family circle. The dog will make life miserable for everyone. This is a dog-person's dog, a handsome and intelligent beast of incredible quality. No less an owner can survive with it.

Chesapeake Bay Retriever: It began, they say, with a shipwreck and ended with an all-American breed of exceptional quality.

In 1807 an English brig encountered heavy seas off the coast of Maryland and foundered. It was clear that she was going down, and luckily for the crew, an American ship, the *Canton*, happened along. The crew of the brig was pulled to safety along with several dogs they had aboard. These included two Newfoundlands: a dingy red dog named Sailor and a black bitch who was renamed Canton after the rescuing vessel. The grateful British sailors gave the two puppies to the men of the *Canton*, and eventually these animals were bred to nondescript retrieving dogs in use around the Chesapeake Bay area, a place of rough, cold winter seas. Some say English Otter Hounds were crossed in—doubtful! Some say yellow Coonhounds—again, doubtful! No one really knows what the incoming blood was, but by 1885, seventy-eight years after the wreck, a dog of a distinct type had emerged. We call it the Chesapeake Bay Retriever.

That dog today can be almost any solid color—dark brown to burnt-grass tan, with or without a white chest spot. The coat is double—woolly underneath, thick and short on top—and about an inch and a half long. The breed's height runs to twenty-six inches, its weight to seventy-four pounds.

The Chesapeake is an altogether superior dog—loyal, smart, affectionate, and a consummate watchdog. Never cranky or petty, he is great with kids. He is stable and ready, forever willing. He is superior in cold weather and will handle water of any temperature, will swim through almost any seas. Solid, positive, clean, and direct in his dealings with people and other animals is the Chesy.

This is, of course, a true Sporting Dog, an outdoor animal, and not one intended for apartment living. Even the suburbs are a question mark unless you are going to exercise your dog regularly. If you have space or if you live an active life, you might want to think about this superior breed of dog. No one has ever regretted owning one. They are for the family with a very big heart and an eternally youthful attitude toward life.

Vizsla: A thousand years ago, the Magyar hordes swept into what is now Hungary. They had a hunting companion, a dog whose name we do not know. The open terrain of agricultural Hungary fostered large hares and plenty of game birds, and a dog was needed that could stand the burning summers and required little cover. Here, then, amid the wheat and corn, the rye and the barley, the Hungarian Pointer or Vizsla was developed, bred by warlords and huntsmen. We think we find its ancestor, looking very much like the Vizsla of today, in ancient manuscripts on falconry. It was a warlike land and a tough world. The Vizsla seemed to satisfy the kind of men who could survive both.

The Vizsla today is medium sized, about twenty-four inches at the withers. He is solid colored—rusty gold or sandy yellow, darker shades preferred, though not dark brown. The coat is short, smooth, dense, without any sign of undercoat. A distinguished-looking dog, the Vizsla has a docked tail and is essentially Pointer style. He is robust, but not at all heavy, has power and drive, and works hard in the field. His back is a little short, and he has a long gait. He is very lightfooted, very smooth, and above all, graceful. He is a keen dog and needs a great deal of exercise every day. He is strictly a country dog, very active, very headstrong, and he requires careful training. He is a natural hunter, and his learning ability is definitely above average. Good-natured by temperament, he will be well mannered when well trained. He is wildly demonstrative at times, and since he is so affectionate, he really has to be handled by someone who knows what the word *master* means. He wants to work, wants to be trained, wants to participate, but he can be a first-class nuisance in the hands of a wishy-washy personality.

The Vizsla is a great family dog where there is land. I know of one specimen that has, on two occasions, leaped through a closed window because he felt he had been left at home alone too long. So I do not see the Vizsla in an apartment, though I do see this splendid and ancient breed very clearly with the yellow grass deep and reflecting on his coat of gold. Strong, fine, well-bred, and full of energy and love, the Vizsla is for special people and should be bought from a specialty breeder only.

English Setter: There was a very handsome bird dog in use about four hundred years ago in England, a cross down from the Spanish Land Spaniels, and the descendant of that classical beauty is the English Setter.

All Setters and Spaniels are down from the original hunting dogs of Spain, and this Setter, the upland animal from England, is one of the most splendid. He stands to twenty-five inches and his weight may run as high as seventy pounds, making for a dog of considerable substance. The coat is long, but flat without curl. It should not be woolly in texture. Colors are mixed: black, white, tan, blue, lemon, orange, liver. Above all, the dog should be beautiful to look at. The profile is square and the muzzle long, much longer than the Spaniel's, and it should have a classic look. The tail is feathered, gracefully sweeping back and only slightly down. That tail, by the way, has always been full; even four centuries ago they didn't dock the Setter's tail as they did the Spaniel's.

It is the disposition and intelligence of the Setter that count most. A properly trained example of the breed is mild and sweet mannered. English Setters are great field dogs, of course—famous as hunters of the upland fields—but they are also pets. Being a pet doesn't seem to interfere with a Setter's ability afield. The breed thrives on affection, indeed can be almost sick when it is lacking. I don't like to see a Setter as a kennel dog. They belong where they are loved—by the fire, by their family.

The Setter is smart, very smart, and takes all kinds of training quickly and well. I don't like to see this dog in the apartment, either, because he needs exercise. A couple of hours a day at least. One has to remember, the English Setter is a hunting dog, a field dog, a dog for the outdoor life.

THE HOUNDS

Beagle: He is neat and compact and apparently rather special, since he is one of the all-time most popular dogs in America. He is also a darned good pet.

You could spend the rest of your life researching the ancient archives for the origin of the Beagle and come up dry. There were similar dogs kept by the Greeks, who in turn passed the tradition along to the Romans, and perhaps the Romans took their packs to England, where there were apparently already hunting Hounds, notably in Wales. Some people say the Setter and the original Spaniel were used to beef up the Welsh Hounds. Others reverse that stand and say that Hounds were used to strengthen the bloodlines of early Setter- and Spaniel-like dogs from Spain. It is likely that both things occurred over a long period of time.

There are two basic kinds of Hounds: the sight Hounds—the Irish Wolfhound and the Borzoi are examples—and the scent Hounds like the Bloodhound and the Beagle. The Beagle is a smart little animal about fifteen inches at the shoulder; he runs about an inch taller in England. The breed came here from England, and the National Beagle Club was formed in 1888. Beagles are shown in regular all-breed shows as well as in specialty shows and field trials.

The Beagle is renowned for speed and endurance and eminent trainability. It is hearty and bright and willing. Many people do keep them in apartments, where they can apparently adapt, but I see them as a field dog, an outside animal working and living the life it was designed to live. I guess that is a personal prejudice. I think it would be cruel to ask a Yorkshire Terrier or a Toy Poodle to live the life of a Beagle, and I am not sure it isn't almost as bad to ask a Beagle to be a Yorkie. However, the Beagle remains close to the top every year in numbers registered with the AKC. Fad dogs come and go, but the Beagle holds its own. A sociable dog, Beagles were bred to run in packs. They do bay most beautifully, and they are hunters at heart. You must keep that in mind. A kind of special dog, the Beagle, with more fans than most movie stars.

Dachshund: Truly, this is a dog for all seasons. He comes in a variety of sizes, from miniature to standard, from five pounds to twenty, and he comes in three coat styles: smooth or short-haired, wirehaired, and long-haired.

The Dachshund is the badger dog of Germany, where *Dachs* means "badger" and where, indeed, something like this short-legged, elongated Terrier and Hound combination was used for hunting badger, and lots of other things as well. Originally bigger, Dachshunds have been bred down as pets. They are almost never used for hunting in this country.

Colors in the Dachshund vary. Solid red is common, and there can be any number of different shades—black with tan spots, chocolate brown with lighter brown spots. The colors stay in the blacks, tans, reds, and richer browns, though. The short-haired variety is lovely and sleek, its coat dense, shiny, and clean. The Wirehaired Dachshund has a hard outer coat with a distinct undercoat, and the long-haired variety is silky like a Setter, soft and glossy. You have all that to choose from.

Although the Dachshund has a Terrier-like personality, it is classed as a Hound (and in fact is largely Hound). It is all spunk and play and personality. It makes a good watchdog and, generally, a super family dog. Its relationship with kids is usually fine, its affection for the family is legendary, and it isn't all that upset with strangers. It may take its time before it's ready for one's lap, but it does come around. Some of the very smallest Miniatures can be a mite tense, but the larger specimens are full of self-confidence and are fine.

Although down from hunting dogs, the Dachshund is pure pet dog today and is near perfect in the apartment. Those short legs mean it gets maximum benefit from a short walk. It is clean, happy, affectionate, and does bark at people on fire escapes and with crowbars. If you want a great family and apartment dog, you can certainly think Dachshund with a good chance of total satisfaction. There is a problem with back trouble in some specimens, actually disc trouble, so keep an eye on your Dachshund, and see your veterinarian from time to time.

Basset Hound: The ever-popular and quite delightful Basset Hound comes from France and Belgium, tradition has it, where for hundreds of years he was used for hunting, trailing, and flushing game. His ancestors were the Bloodhound and the St. Hubert Hound, and he is second only to the pure Bloodhound in scenting ability.

Having spent most of his years as a breed in the company of man afield, often working in packs, the Basset Hound comes down to us as a docile, friendly, and easily trained dog. He is intelligent and characteristically loyal. He is one of the most difficult of dogs to ruffle. He can live with anyone or anything, and in the home situation, he is marvelous with children. His reputation for being a one-man dog is only partly deserved. He is so malleable that if raised as a one-man dog, that is what he will be, but if raised in a family, he will be a family dog. The Basset is as you would have him.

His short legs were, of course, evolved to aid him in pursuit of game in dense cover, and his incredible nose is a magical device. Those long ears were developed to stir up scent—as the Hound sweeps the land, his ears dangle and swirl lingering fragments of scent that have settled and might otherwise be missed. The Basset was originally a country dog (hunting, at least the kind that requires a scent Hound, being limited as an urban activity), and he is still at his best in the country. He can, however, adapt to apartment life as long as he is walked at least three or four times a day. He needs that exercise and should be considered a pet only if one can be certain in advance that he will get it.

The Basset is a healthy dog and not at all given to digestive difficulties. He isn't a fussy eater unless you make him that way. His only problem centers on his ears. They dangle and get scratched and scraped and can develop sore tips. A Basset's ears should be checked regularly.

A lovely, whimsical, comic-book character of a dog to look at, a gentleman, a companion, a loving friend to live with, the Basset is all of these. See a specialty breeder, and think about the Basset. Your family will love you for it.

Afghan Hound: Heaven only knows why anyone would want to own a so-called exotic pet when there are dogs like this around. The Afghan Hound should be exotic enough for anyone, bank president to belly dancer. The origins of this breed trace back to Egypt between five and six thousand years ago. The Afghan was a favorite of royalty then, as a hunting and coursing dog. He is what is called a sight Hound. Adapted for the hilly terrain of Afghanistan, he was used to hunt leopards, which should tell you something about his nerve.

The Afghan is acceptable in any color, but the coat is always thick and silky and has a fine texture. Afghanistan has terrible extremes of weather, and the Afghan

Hound was developed to tolerate all of them, burning summers to frozen winters. He is twenty-eight inches tall, weighs between sixty and sixty-five pounds, and is all stamina; like all sight Hounds, he can push on for hours. His high hips make him a superb jumper, and he is fantastic going uphill. Even walking on a sidewalk, this animal immediately attracts attention, for he appears to float, to levitate with each step. His movement, I believe, is the most beautiful in the dog world. When he opens up and runs, the sight is beyond description. The Afghan in motion is poetry, nothing less.

With a background of mountains in Afghanistan and hunting leopards, can this dog make a good pet? Surprisingly, yes. He is almost never ill-tempered, almost always gentle and pleasant. He takes his time when it comes to new people and has the reputation of being reserved, but then gentlemen usually are. He is loyal to his master and a lover of his home. He won't attack the friendly stranger, but he will be slow in sharing his affection.

No one should even think of owning an Afghan Hound unless he or she is prepared for exercise. It is criminal to deny this dog an opportunity to move, hours each day. He doesn't have to have leopards to chase, nor does he need the hills of Afghanistan, but he does need long, long walks every day, in all weather. He should get regular opportunities to run, to open up and lay flat out in that field of clover. The Afghan is an expensive dog; he is a beautiful, even a stunning animal. He is a conversation piece and a love affair. Think Afghan if you like walking.

Norwegian Elkhound: By all counts, the magnificent Norwegian Elkhound is one of the greatest breeds of dog ever developed by man. He goes back almost seven thousand years, and his bones have been found with those of his Viking masters.

The twenty-inch-tall, fifty-pound Elkhound from Norway is one of the oldest forms of purebred dog; and he is as he was, virtually unchanged. He evolved from himself, style dictated by need, and it is only by good luck, really, that he is a handsome dog, for need and function came first. He is one of the most rugged of all dogs. No weather can bother him, he has stamina if not speed, and he has brains. He can learn anything and is always loyal. He has been a worker, a hunting Hound, a guard dog, a companion; he sailed on Viking ships, he guarded Viking camps, he scaled mountains, herded sheep and cattle, fought wolves and bears, retrieved, pointed, held big game at bay, and he played with children in camps and small rustic villages. And we have him today as they had him then, before England was England, before Christ, perhaps as much as five thousand years before the beginning of the Christian era.

The Norwegian Elkhound is probably the same color now he always was, shades of gray, lighter below, with black tips. The coat, as one might expect, is thick and hard. The head is well cut and handsome. The body is square, the ears are prick and alert, the tail is curled up and over. The Norwegian Elkhound is a smart dog, with senses so good they border on intuition. He can hear and smell things, they say, two or three miles away. This could be the world's perfect watchdog. He is a ready barker with a high-pitched bark, one that will carry and be heard.

The fiercely loyal, friendly, and willing Elkhound also has a mind of his own. He is to be owned by strong-minded people who will be masters and who will direct that energy. He needs supervision, because he can be aggressive. There is nothing this dog can't adapt to, no situation he can't master and learn to enjoy. Personally, though, I do not see the Norwegian Elkhound in the apartment or in the city. This is a large, robust, and powerful outdoor dog for outdoor people. A high point in dogdom is the ancient and magnificent Norwegian Elkhound.

Basenji: The Basenji is a marvelous little Hound of very ancient lineage. The pharaohs of Egypt got these dogs as gifts, brought down in tribute from the sources of the Nile. The breed originated in central Africa thousands of years ago, and nothing at all is known about its original bloodline. They were first seen in England in 1895; those dogs died of distemper, and not until 1937 was the breed seen in the United States. A pair was brought in and bred, but the bitch and the puppies all died, again of distemper. Eventually, though, the dog was successfully bred here, and AKC registration came in 1943.

The Basenji is close to Fox Terrier size, about seventeen inches, and weighs twenty-four pounds. Its coat is short and extremely silky and shiny. It fairly glistens in the sun. Colors are preferably deep chestnut red or pure black, or black and tan with white feet, chest, and tail tip. White legs, blaze, and collar are allowed. The Basenji is often called the barkless dog, and it is true that they don't bark like ordinary dogs. They do have a kind of chortling yodel, but it is reserved for those they love. It is a sound of greeting and affection. They have a variety of other noises, too.

The Basenji is as clean as a cat, cleaning itself all over *like* a cat with great regularity. Quiet, small, and clean, Basenjis are perfect for the apartment. They are proud, very affectionate, and they love children. They have a marvelous gait and look handsome on a leash. They adapt to any weather, hot or cold, and want to be in on everything the family does. They are attention-getters with their pointed ears, deep, dark eyes, frown marks, glistening coat, and curled tail. In dog shows, they always draw a crowd. This is still a relatively little-known dog, but one that is bound to become more and more popular as time goes on. If you live in limited space and want happiness on four legs, think about the lover from the Congo lands, the little Hound called Basenji.

Borzoi: Here is a dog that is elegant above all others, a true aristocrat. Until 1936, the name for this dog was Russian Wolfhound, but since that time, Borzoi has been preferred. These large, expensive, and superbly elegant creatures are Hounds. They came from Russia, where they were used for coursing the wolf.

Coursing with sight Hounds goes far back into history. There were Gazelle Hounds in the ancient world, the Greyhounds and the Saluki probably go back to Sumeria seven thousand years ago, and Genghis Khan liked the sport in the thirteenth century. All of this history is packed into the stately Borzoi.

Back in the 1600s, a Russian duke is said to have imported Arabian Greyhounds, but they could not stand the weather and died off. He tried again and crossed them with a Russian herding dog not unlike the Collie. This line survived, tradition has it, and gave rise to the Wolfhound. No doubt other Russian Hound blood contributed, and today's animal may well carry a tiny bit of blood from the dogs of the Mongol hordes.

The Borzoi stands to thirty-one inches at the shoulder and can weigh 105 pounds. It is one of the giant dogs, one of the tallest there is. The coat is long and silky and all colors are allowed, although white usually predominates. Speed is the main characteristic of this breed, speed and stamina. Borzoi run in packs. They can run almost any wild animal to earth, and once on to a quarry, they are hard to call back. Some citizens of our western states are running down coyotes with packs of Borzoi. It is not a pretty sight, not something of which we should be particularly proud.

You see Borzoi being walked in city parks today, and they are something to look at. Still, one wonders about keeping a massive coursing Hound in a city apartment, and I personally think they are better owned in pairs. So, one wonders about two or more of them in an apartment. Seems to me like a cross of masochism and sadism. I guess they can take it, though, as long as they are walked hours every day. When you see a pair go by, watch the motion. Even in a casual walk, it is like seeing something solid flow like liquid.

Irish Wolfhound: A great many people want more than just a dog, they want a pet. They want meaning, too, a sense of history. All of that is in the tallest, strongest dog in the world, the Irish Wolfhound.

The mists of history have the whole story, and they will not share it with us, but we do know that when the Celts sacked Delphi in 273 B.C., they had with them what were probably Irish Wolfhounds. The Roman consul Quintus Aurelius Symmachus wrote to his brother Flavianus and thanked him for some specimens that were used, true to Roman style, as gladiators in the circuses. All through history in fact, from ancient to modern times, the Irish Wolfhound appears. A Spanish poet wrote an ode to this breed; kings are said to have fought over examples. They were sold, presented, stolen, ransomed—we will never know what is fact and what is fiction, so much has been said and written.

The Irish Wolfhound stands to thirty-three inches at the shoulder and weighs 140 pounds. He is built for speed, stamina, and enormous strength. The coat is very rough and wiry and colors vary—brindle gray, black, red, white, tan. I personally like gray, and that color is in fact generally preferred.

The loyalty of this animal is part of the legend, and it is also part of the fact. The Irish Wolfhound is generally a sweet-mannered animal unless there is a threat to his people, then beware, for this animal will tackle anything and probably win. He is dignified, sure, self-contained, not petty, not nervous, and is the perfect guard and a grand companion. How about children? Fine. He seems to have a sure sense of how to handle himself around little people. Some owners keep these dogs in an apartment, and I am afraid I can't see that. This is not only the tallest dog in the world, it is an outdoor animal, born and bred to guard, to roam and run. They can't roam anymore, of course, but they do need exercise, as do all sight Hounds. A super dog for folks with land, he is a magnificent guard on the farm, for he does not have to be guard trained—it is built in. He settles into a home for life and takes care of it, people and all. This is truly superdog. Buy only from the best breeders, people who worship this breed and care about every puppy born.

Bloodhound: When we hear this dog's name spoken, we immediately conjure up images of fleeing felons and pursuing dogs. There is an undeserved quality of merci-lessness to that image, for the Bloodhound is gentle and pleasant. Remember, it isn't used to hurt man, only follow him, and it is used to find lost children as often as to locate escaped convicts.

The ancestry of this remarkable scent Hound traces back to ancient Egypt, Greece, and Rome. They are called Bloodhounds not because they are bloody, but because it was blooded people, nobility, who used to own them. They came to Europe from Constantinople and were written about as far back as the third century A.D. They are famous for their noses, of course; they are not killers, as we have said, but followers. They are gentle animals, even tender, and are just great with children. Their somber looks make them a delight to have around, and they have a stoic quality that makes them good baby-sitters. They are not fighters and are good with all other animals once they get to know them. They need an enormous amount of exercise to keep in condition. For that reason, they are not good apartment dogs, but belong in a very active, physical environment; perfect on the farm or out in the country.

The colors are limited, black and tan, red and tan, or a kind of tawny. The coat is thin and loose. The dog may stand to twenty-seven inches at the withers and weigh as much as 110 pounds. Either sex is a fine pet animal in the right setting. Never buy a Bloodhound from a pet dealer, only from a breeder. Pride in this breed by people who have devoted their lives to it is immense. They don't want their dogs in the hands of people who won't share that pride and match it with love and care. No breeder of Bloodhounds wants to think of one of his puppies misused or ill cared for.

Whippet: There is no more elegant dog than the Whippet, none more decorative, and none more ideal for life in the house or apartment. They are both intelligent and graceful. They have been called Miniature English

Greyhounds, Snap-dogs, and other things as well, but Whippet is the name. Every Whippet looks like a piece of French porcelain, or like a character from an ancient tapestry on a museum wall. I personally have never seen a Whippet look ungraceful or lacking elegance.

This coursing Hound from England—with Greyhound and perhaps some Terrier and Italian Greyhound blood—is only a little more than a century old, but over that century, it has graced some of the most discerning dog-owning homes in the world. Our Whippet today stands to twenty-two inches and weighs to twenty-eight pounds, although often as much as ten pounds below that.

Whippets are bright, cheerful, gentle, and seldom snappy. I have known a good number and have never known one with a mean streak. They are extremely affectionate and loyal, love approval, and they love to play even after full maturity. They are the fastest dog in the world in their size class, and can do over thirty-five miles an hour. For this reason, because they are such fine athletes, they do need exercise. Even just a visit to the park will do, so that they can run and run and run in circles. To watch them, you would think their hearts would burst, then you realize they are just warming up to the game.

Whippets are easy to train, one of the easiest of all dogs. They can be housebroken in a couple of days. They are hardy, despite what some people regard as a fragile appearance, they are not fussy eaters, and they are easy to keep clean. The coat is short, hard, and quite firm. They can be any color, but most often they are gray, tan, and/or white.

The Whippet is a house dog, a pet dog, a very close and intimate friend, and that is the way he should be kept. Whippets are fine with kids, just fine. When all things are taken into account, you would have to rate this breed very near the top of the list of dogdom. This is the classic beauty and the perfect pet. Don't buy a Whippet from anyone but the specialty breeder of repute. This dog must be bred and raised through his early and impressionable weeks by someone who worships the breed above all others.

THE WORKING BREEDS

German Shepherd Dog: With this dog's lines descending from the herding farm dogs of old, the name German *Police* Dog is clearly a misnomer. This handsome and intelligent animal stands to twenty-five inches and weighs as much as eighty-five pounds, although bitches may be trim and natural at sixty pounds. The accepted colors are black and tan, gray, or black. The coat is double, protective, harsh, straight, and close-lying.

The German Shepherd is a noble-looking animal, smart, quick, and sure. It is loyal and brave, a friend for life. The breed has an excellent nose and is as quick to learn as any breed of dog. They are used to guide the blind, of course, although not as exclusively as was once the case. They make excellent police dogs and guard dogs when properly trained. They are naturally fine pets and very assertive watchdogs.

Why then all the fear? Why the reports from plastic surgeons that eighty percent of their dog-bite repairs are caused by German Shepherd attacks? The main reason for the apparent contradiction over this noble dog is the poor breeders and unscrupulous trainers who sell half-trained animals as defenders of the home. A guard-trained Shepherd, much less an attack-trained Shepherd, belongs in the average homeowner's grasp about as much as does a loaded Luger. The German Shepherd is a powerful and intelligent animal. When that power and intelligence are bent by some foolish breeder or trainer, that is when those horrifying statistics get compounded. Never, *never* buy a German Shepherd from anyone but the original breeder. Meet the parents of the puppy you are considering, and, because the breed is very prone to hip dysplasia, insist that X rays be made of the pup's hips at an age suggested by a veterinarian. Because the German Shepherd has been so extremely popular, there are scores of totally unprofessional, unscrupulous breeders mass-producing these animals for sale to pet shops and puppy mills. Don't be trapped. If you are thinking of the super-intelligent and super-loyal German Shepherd, see the best breeder you can find, the kind that only has this one breed of dog.

Doberman Pinscher: The Doberman Pinscher was developed in Germany around 1890 by a gentleman named Louis Doberman. It is said to be a mixture of Black-and-Tan Terrier, German Pinscher, and Rottweiler. This magnificent breed stands to twenty-eight inches, weighs to seventy-five pounds, and has a sleek, hard, close coat. Colors are black and brown.

The Doberman is certainly a loyal and affectionate animal, and a superb watchdog. It wants to serve its family. But a lot of people fear Dobermans. Is that fear justified? The AKC standard book bears this notation near the top of the Doberman standards: "The judge shall dismiss from the ring any shy or vicious Doberman." It defines viciousness this way: "A dog that attacks or attempts to attack either the judge or its handler is definitely vicious. An aggressive or belligerent attitude towards other dogs shall not be deemed viciousness." Rarely in the standards does the AKC find it necessary to make statements like these.

The Doberman can be a problem for the less-than-really-skilled owner. The person who takes on a Doberman had better be assertive and in full command at all times. A Doberman off the leash can be murder on other pets, for few animals can withstand the assault of one of these magnificent, sleek athletes of the dog world. I should think a Doberman Pinscher would be about as good a canine friend and protector as you could want, but you had better be absolutely sure that you are capable of keeping your charge from becoming the Genghis Khan of your neighborhood. The Doberman Pinscher is not the casual owner's dog, and the traveling salesman who thinks he will sleep better while on the road if his wife has a Doberman Pinscher with her had better take himself, wife, and dog to obedience school beforehand. This is a special breed of dog and should only be in the hands of special owners. As for kids, I'm not sure. I have known some Dobermans that were dolls and some that were terrors. A lot depends on the individual dog and his individual owner-trainer. As for guard-trained or attack-trained Doberman Pinschers, forget it. Not for the private citizen. And never buy one of these sleek beauties from anyone but a top specialty breeder.

Collie: Once upon a time, in the Highlands, they called them Coally dogs, and that is where the name Collie comes from.

Sheepherding is one of man's oldest professions, and so the origins of the herding Collie go far back in time, just how far or to where we don't know. There are two varieties of the Collie today: the rough-coated (the one most often seen in this country) and the smooth-coated. Back in the 1880s, we know, Roughs and Smooths were coming from the same litter, but that is not so now.

The Collie is one of the most refined of all purebred dogs, and a good specimen is a thing of great beauty. Taller now than he was in the last century, the Collie dog can stand to twenty-six inches and weigh seventy-five pounds. Colors are sable and white, blue merle, white, black, tan, or any combination. The coat is straight and tends to have a harsh texture; in the Rough Collie it is very thick and long. The Collie is an intelligent dog, a Working Dog, a hardy and loyal dog with natural guarding instincts. That makes the breed fine with kids and fine as watchdogs. But some specimens may prove to be too highly bred, especially in this country. That can make them tense, so be careful, and don't get a nervous Collie. The pup should be relaxed, bright, and friendly. A Collie isn't always the most trustful dog in the world when it comes to strangers, but for members of the family, no dog was ever more loyal. The Collie is not a dog for the indoors. He has been bred to spend most of his life outside, and there just isn't enough bad weather around to bother him. The Collie needs exercise and brushing. Seriously, no one should consider this breed, at least in the rough-coated variety, unless they intend to brush the dog hard and long every single day of its life. Then and only then will that coat shine and show its splendor. And such grooming is not just for looks. Like all long-coated dogs, the Collie is subject to skin troubles and parasites, and brushing is more than a beauty treatment, it is a step to good health.

Don't ever buy a Collie from anyone but a professional breeder. Collies have been so popular for so long that some perfectly dreadful strains are around from the mass-production boys. Only get a Collie from someone who really loves and knows the breed. Only then will you be satisfied, and no one is more satisfied than a satisfied Collie owner.

Shetland Sheepdog: By all standards, the Shetland Sheepdog (or Sheltie) is a superdog. There are varying theories about original blood, but there can be little doubt that the Hill Collies of old Scotland somehow got out to the Shetland Islands and there bred down in size, in the way of all domestic animals on those islands. (From there came, after all, the Shetland pony, as well as some of the smallest breeds of sheep and cattle known.)

The Shetland Sheepdog is a worker, hardy like all Shetlanders, obedient by nature, and positively super as a watchdog. That trait is built into the breed, as is the need to please. The Sheltie wants to make everybody happy.

The coat is long and quite straight. It has a characteristically harsh texture and colors vary: all kinds of combinations of black, blue merle, gold, mahogany. Heights run to sixteen inches in the dog and weights to as many pounds. The bitch isn't much smaller, generally.

The Sheltie loves his family and is good with strangers once they are shown to be no threat to the homestead. This is one Working Dog that is fine in an apartment. He does, however, have one small drawback: the Sheltie can be a ragged mess unless brushed with vigor and purpose. That lovely coat is made to look that way by attention, it doesn't just happen. People who have limited living space, but who love that sensible Working Dog quality, should consider the Sheltie.

Fanciers don't like the comparison, and I can understand their point, but the Shetland Sheepdog really is a

Collie in miniature. There is probably some Spaniel in him as well as Collie, but he does have that striking resemblance and the many other lovely qualities of the Collie of old. Shelties are bright, loyal, graceful creatures, and they do have a sense of humor, I don't care what anyone says. They don't go around cracking jokes, it's true, but they have a way about them that shows a special and quite enviable zest for life.

St. Bernard: His history is the most romantic of all, yet there is much we do not know about the great Swiss hospice dog, the St. Bernard. The ancestor of the St. Bernard may have been the Molossian-type dog brought to Europe from Asia by returning Roman armies. If that is the case, then this ancestor was introduced to the Swiss Alps at about the time of Christ. Still, the connection is conjecture.

Until about 1830, all St. Bernards were short-haired, but then, when disease and inbreeding seemed about to destroy the breed, the monks of the Hospice of St. Bernard crossed in Newfoundland blood. The St. Bernard continued true, but now as a longer-haired strain. The St. Bernard coat is extremely dense and lies against the body. Colors are usually combinations of white and red, and there can be darker markings on the head. This is a large dog, to twenty-nine inches and to 180 pounds.

The ability of the St. Bernard to follow a trail and maintain direction is uncanny. They were bred for and used to save travelers in the Alps, as the stories go, and all the qualities you might expect in such an animal are there. The Saint is steady and durable, and there just isn't any weather that will bother him. He is clearly not an apartment dog. He belongs outside, although he should, of course, have a shelter where he can get dry. Don't leave him in the rain.

The St. Bernard is usually gentle, even-tempered, and loyal. He responds well to kindness, to honest affection. He can be marvelous with children. I have known only two St. Bernards in my life that weren't placid; one of them had been trained to guard a gas station, and the other was just a lousy example of the breed.

Characteristically, the St. Bernard is a pleasure to have around the outside of the house. (They drool a great deal, and who needs that on the carpet.) As is true with all large dogs, one that misbehaves is a monumental pest, and there is simply no reason to let that happen. This breed is easy to train and is willing to learn and live by the rules. Judging from the experiences of several St. Bernard owning friends, once you own one of these magnificent dogs, you will never want to be without one or two. Just be certain you know what you are getting into and that you have the room for a horse-sized dog. Also be certain to buy only from the finest of specialty breeders. Poor examples can turn out to be dangerous, particularly males over five years of age.

Siberian Husky: No one knows how long the Siberian Husky has been a pure strain, but it is certainly a matter of centuries, perhaps many centuries. The Chukchi people of northeastern Asia developed the breed as a companion, as a family guard dog and sled dog. Almost two feet tall, sixty pounds, with a dense double coat in almost any color plus white, and with that characteristic heart-shaped marking on the face, they are stunning animals.

More than some other sled-type dogs, Huskies are kind and gentle and extremely affectionate. They are usually wonderful with children and seem to be able to adapt to any family situation. They came to the attention of the general public in 1925, when the Alaskan city of Nome was stricken with a diphtheria epidemic. Dog teams were used to bring lifesaving vaccine to the affected area, and among them was a superb team driven by Leonhard Seppala. After the Nome episode was over, Seppala toured America with his dogs. They caught on. Within five years, the breed had a following of its own and AKC recognition. That was in 1930. They have become steadily more popular since and are almost certainly the most popular of the large sled dogs today, down here below the Arctic.

Any negative qualities? Yes, a few. Huskies will wander unless trained early and very well. They have been known to worry livestock, so there is that to train out of them as well. And they do shed like the very devil. In the spring, you can pull fistfuls of fur out of them. They really must be stripped expertly or kept outside once the weather turns warm. (I have heard of a woman who will take your Husky fur, if you save it as it is shed, and will spin and weave it for you.)

No doubt, the Husky, a hardy, handsome outdoor dog, is one of the most adaptable of Working breeds. Some people keep them in apartments, but they are better outside and better in colder climates. They are stunning and very pleasant animals, but can be clowns and awful babies if given a chance.

Great Dane: There is something special about anything that is really big—call it the romance of giants—and that is true of a giant dog like the majestic Great Dane.

Despite his name, the Great Dane comes from Germany, not Denmark. His history may trace back as far as two thousand years. He could be the descendant of the Tiger dog of ancient Egypt. It seems fairly certain that the Saxons brought ancestors of the Dane to England for boar hunting, and that would explain the dog's large size, boar hunting being heavy work. But the Great Dane is not considered a hunting or Sporting Dog today. He is rated a Working Dog.

A Dane can stand as high as thirty-four inches at the shoulder and can weigh up to 150 pounds. The coat is glossy and short. Colors range through the brindles, tans, and fawns—even blue is seen—but my favorites are the spectacular black-and-white dogs known as Harlequins.

When picking a pet, you should take your home situation into consideration. Are you prepared to house and care for a dog almost three feet tall at the shoulder and the weight of a man? The Dane is playful, and while usually gentle, he isn't always the best animal to have around a toddler. Wait until your kid can hold his own against a mountain of moving dog. I don't see the Dane as an apartment dog, unless your apartment is barn sized. He needs exercise and should only be maintained in situations where he can get it without jumping over your coffee table. As to cost? Plan on spending $175 for an average specimen; if you are considering a show animal, think, would you believe, at least $600. However good his disposition, a Dane will certainly turn off any burglar casing your house. That's in his favor. Also not to be overlooked is the feeling of pleasure and pride a man, woman, or child can get from walking a dog like a Dane. But anyone who buys a dog that weighs 150 pounds has a responsibility to everyone around him to see that it is equipped to live among people. No one has the right to a badly behaved dog, least of all one the size of a Great Dane.

Old English Sheepdog: The Old English Sheepdog isn't an old breed. The first depiction of one was by Gainsborough in a painting dated 1771. We don't know the parent stock. The breed apparently came from the west of England, from Devon, Somerset, and Cornwall. Parent stock could have been the Bearded Collie, as some people believe, or even the Russian Owtchar, as others say. We will never know.

The Old English Sheepdog today stands to twenty-five inches and weighs up to sixty-five pounds. With that coat it looks very much larger. The coat is profuse, to say the least, with a hard texture, and is shaggy but not curly. Colors run gray, grizzle, blue, and blue merle, with or without white. The whole appearance of the dog should be square and blocky. The coat isn't as much trouble as one might think. One good brisk brushing every day should do it.

The Old English Sheepdog (which isn't all that old) is a Working Dog and should be active. I do not agree with some people that it is a good apartment dog. It is too agile, too active; it can go a little stir crazy. Sheepdogs are fantastic on a farm or in open areas where they can move much of each day and with that wonderful bearlike rolling shuffle of a gait. They are fine with cattle and, of course, sheep. They are great pets and generally wonderful with children. They are intelligent and responsive and easygoing with strangers. Back to apartment living; you must accept that that is a personal opinion. I have known more than a few that were kept in apartments, and I found them not to be the dog they should be. Maybe that was because they came from puppy mills and were poor examples anyway, or maybe it was because they were cooped up. Perhaps both. My advice would be, buy only from a good specialty breeder, and buy for the home with

plenty of room. Great if there are kids handy to run
with the dog; he and they will love it.

Boxer: Here is a handsome dog with outstanding qualities and of ancient lineage. The Boxer is down, no
doubt, from some ancient dog of Tibet, and in him has
gone Terrier, Bulldog, and some people think even a
little Great Dane.

The Boxer is a tough Working Dog from Germany
that reached its present perfection during the last century. Before then, although the Boxer idea was there,
he was a different and cruder-looking animal. Today's
Boxer stands to twenty-four inches and weighs as much
as seventy-five pounds. This is a strong, muscular animal. The coat is short and smooth and shiny when the
animal is healthy. Colors run fawn and brindle, usually
but not always marked with white. The overall impression is one of power—solid, full assertive power—and
agility. The breed was used for police work, and that,
no doubt, had a lot to do with the way it developed.

The Boxer is a sensational pet—clean, affectionate,
loyal to the death. It is usually great with kids, a clown
that loves to romp when things are peaceful, and a
watchdog to reckon with if danger appears to threaten
the household; the bitch is as good as the dog in this
regard. The Boxer can be quarrelsome with other dogs
and cats, not always by any means, but it can be
something of a problem, so all Boxers should undergo
obedience training just to insure their behavior as nice-
mannered family members. Boxers like being with people, going where people go, and for that privilege they
should be under control at all times and know how
to behave. There is no more monumental pest in this
world than an aggressive, uncontrolled, ill-mannered

Boxer; and no finer pet, no better friend than a Boxer who knows how to mind.

By all means, think about a Boxer. And be sure to buy yours only from a specialty breeder. The mass-producers really have made a mess of this one. And do train your Boxer to live among people. He will love you for it.

Samoyed: People who speak favorably of this dog do not do so in modest terms. They say it is the most beautiful of all dogs, they say it is the truest of all dogs, and they say it is the best natured. The Samoyed is a dog that really excites people.

When they speak of the Samoyed being true, they mean it is pure dog, close to the primitive ancestor. The Samoyed comes from the eastern shore of the White Sea in Russia and takes his name from the Samoyed people, migratory keepers of reindeer. The dog and this people have been together for thousands of years, and it is firmly believed that the dog we know today has been exactly the same for all of that time.

The people who say it is the most beautiful of all dogs will have to fight for that claim, but their favorite is magnificent. The male weighs sixty-five pounds and is almost two feet tall. It is generally all white, but can be biscuit and white-and-biscuit; no other colors are allowed. The coat is straight, long, and extremely dense. This breed can, of course, tolerate any extreme low temperature and indeed is happiest in cold climates. He isn't a dog I would pick to live on the equator.

There is simply nothing wrong with the Samoyed. He is happy, loyal, and affectionate. He is so good-natured it just doesn't seem possible, and he is fantastic with kids, whimsical with a positive sense of humor.

The Sam isn't a fighter. He is gentle and kind and

very smart. He can live in the house, he can live out of doors. Until you have romped with one in knee-deep snow, as I have on occasion, you can't appreciate what a truly magnificent creature is available here for the discerning dog owner. Truly, it is hard to find a breed as close to perfect as the Samoyed. Their beauty and high style, their attention-attracting qualities make for pride in the owner, while all of their other qualities provide the warm feelings a dog perfectly integrated into the family can give. I would pay this breed the ultimate compliment. The Samoyed is on a par with the Golden Retriever.

Newfoundland: Just how the great Newfoundland originated is not clear. Everyone seems to agree that Basque fishermen arriving on Newfoundland brought dogs with them (some say they were Great Pyrenees), and these were crossed with Huskies and some French dogs, most notably Hounds. From the mixture, whatever it was, the Newfoundland emerged. Eventually, the breed was perfected in England and returned to Newfoundland a fait accompli.

The Newfoundland is a massive animal, to twenty-eight inches and 150 pounds. The color is black with an occasional tinge of bronze and a white chest mark. The coat is dense and double. It is also oily and the toes are webbed, for this is a water dog, a natural lifesaver, and indeed the incidents of this great animal pulling men, women, and children from icy seas are legendary.

Because this splendid dog is pony-sized, it is not for the apartment, but it is for just about every other human situation you can imagine. Newfoundlands are natural watchdogs, natural baby-sitters, they love kids and other animals, and generally are as sweet and gentle as they are huge. They are extremely affectionate with their own family, and very tolerant of other people once they are sure their family is not endangered. They have been used as working dogs on Newfoundland—pulling carts, helping to haul nets, doing anything a heavy-boned, well-muscled dog would do—so they are very hardy. It is difficult to imagine a quality you would want in a dog that is not found in the Newfoundland, except lap size.

I think it is a mistake to try and force this animal into a situation without ample room, for adaptable as it is, it cannot make itself shrink. If it could it would, I am sure, for that is how willing they are. If you have the room, and especially if you live an active life (for this is a dog that likes action and needs daily exercise), think about one of the truly great dogs, the splendid black Newfoundland.

Alaskan Malamute: No one really knows where the people came from—Asia, Greenland, Hudson Bay, some place north of Europe, perhaps—but they called themselves *innuit. Innuit* means "people," *the* people being implied. And among the *innuit*, there was a special group. The early North American explorers, the first people to encounter them, referred to them as "high-type" *innuit*. They were happy, pleasant, well organized, and superb hunters, and they were kinder to their dogs than any of the other northern natives that had so far been discovered by Europeans. No one ever talked about these special *innuit* without mentioning their dogs and the incredible bond the people had with them. The name of the special *innuit*? Mahlemuts. That became bastardized over the years to Malamutes, and that is the name we have for their dogs today.

Some people mistakenly refer to this dog as a Husky, and that is wrong. The Husky comes from Siberia. The mistake may have come from the fact that in the *innuit* language, the Orarian language to be exact, *husky* is a slangy insult meaning something like "slob."

Today's Alaskan Malamute stands to twenty-five inches and weighs up to eighty-five pounds. His coat is thick and coarse to the touch; it should never be soft. Colors are wolf gray or black and white. This is a powerful, handsome, stable, and loyal dog and should never be petty or mean. He should be friendly and willing, but not overbearing. He can be a very good watchdog, and he makes a fine pet. He loves miserable weather—outside is fine with him. This is a dog, however, with more than a little wolf in him, and he needs a firm, steady master or mistress who will not give ground. He is what we call a Spitz-type dog, but there is no doubt about the wolf. They say that the northern people tether their bitches out on the ice when they are in heat and let the wolves come to them in the night. True? I don't know.

I knew one team of Malamutes that belonged to a New Zealand exploration team in the Antarctic, and what magnificent dogs they were. Several generations of them were born on the ice and had never seen the inside of a building. The temperature went to almost one hundred below zero, and the winds could be way over a hundred miles an hour. When the dogs curled up and were snowed over, do you know how you could tell where they were after the storm had passed? They would wag their tails at the sound of your approach, and that would disturb the snow above them. A great dog, the Alaskan Malamute, from a great and fearless northern people.

Pembroke Welsh Corgi: The Pembroke Welsh Corgi is a dog of character and quality. For quick reference, how do you tell at a glance whether you are looking at a Cardigan Welsh Corgi or a Pembroke Welsh Corgi? The Cardigan has the visible tail, the Pembroke does not.

The Pembroke weighs up to twenty-four pounds and stands to a foot at the withers. Colors run to red, sable, fawn, black-and-tan, with white on the legs, chest, and neck. The breed is newer than the Cardigan Corgi and was brought to Wales by French weavers. It dates back to the twelfth century at least and, again unlike the Cardigan, does not have Dachshund blood. There was some interbreeding of the two Corgi types in the last century and in the beginning of this, and thus the resemblance today.

The Pembroke has an easy-to-care-for coat that is dense and of medium length. It is, in fact, an easy dog to keep. The Pembroke is a natural for the farm and is fine around horses and other stock. It is alert and intelligent, with built-in protective instincts—protective of animals and especially children—and is thus an ideal watchdog. Leave one with a child in a crib or carriage, and, you can depend on it, the child is guarded.

The Pembroke is a tough little dog, full of spirit, active, and "with it." It is affectionate and dependable and wants to participate in everything its human family does. The breed is very long-lived—seventeen or eighteen years is not unusual—is naturally healthy, and can take any weather.

Pembroke Corgis are fine in the apartment as long as they get exercise. Long walks several times a day should be considered a basic condition for ownership. No one should get involved with this breed if long walks are onerous. You should keep your Pembroke Welsh Corgi busy. Romps with rubber balls and similar games are much appreciated. Fine in an apartment, great in the suburbs, lovely on a farm, the Welsh Corgi we call Pembroke is a really fine breed to be obtained only from a fine specialty breeder.

THE TERRIERS

Miniature Schnauzer: There is confusion in many minds as to where the Schnauzer fits in in the scheme of purebred dogs. The Giant Schnauzer, a great dog that goes to twenty-seven and a half inches, and the Standard Schnauzer, a dog that goes to nineteen and a half inches, are both shown in this country as Working Dogs. The Miniature Schnauzer, a breed that goes to fourteen inches, is shown as a Terrier (not as a Toy, as so many people seem to believe).

The Miniature Schnauzer runs in several colors, with black the only solid color allowed. It is seen as salt and pepper and as black and silver. All manner of shades of gray are allowed under the salt-and-pepper heading, including some tan shading. The original Schnauzers were derived in Germany from Poodle and Spitz mixtures and some very old German Pinscher lines. The Miniature was derived from that basic stock by crossing the emerging Schnauzer with the Toy Affenpinscher. At least that is what is generally accepted as the origin of the breed today.

The Miniature is generally less aggressive than either the Standard or the Giant Schnauzer and makes a first-rate pet. Crosses between the Miniature and either of the larger breeds are not allowed. The Miniature is fine, really exceptional with children, and loves to play and be fussed over. It is, in fact, a child itself. The breed is characteristically very intelligent and wants to participate in everything the family does. It does not like being left alone, and it does not like being excluded. A Miniature Schnauzer is something of a commitment —yet one more breed that should not be owned by casual dog owners. It is stylish and smart and bright and belongs in the home of really dog-oriented people.

The breed rated eighth in popularity in America in 1975, and the dreadful midwestern bulk breeders have had a field day shipping examples east and west by the crate. Buy only from the very best breeder, for there are some perfectly dreadful examples of this breed around. The Miniature Schnauzer may have the cutest face and the most alert expression in all of dogdom. A lot of people insist that it does. Whether it is your breed or not, the Miniature Schnauzer is a special kind of dog.

Scottish Terrier: He stands about ten inches at the shoulder and weighs about twenty-two pounds, and he'll dine on rattlesnakes and spar with dragons for relaxation. He is a Terrier through and through. He is the Scottie, the tough Scottish Terrier.

The coat of the Scottie is hard and wiry. The color is often black, although there are brindled, grizzled, sandy, wheaten, and gray examples of the breed. No white markings are allowed by show standards. Those so-called white Scotties are not Scotties at all, but Westies, West Highland White Terriers, and we will discuss them elsewhere.

The Scottie has been shown in England since 1879, but we don't know much about his earlier history. In Perthshire, in an area known as the Blackmount region, there was a breed known as the Old Highland Terrier, and the Scottie may be descended from that dog.

Many breeds of dogs have their avid fanciers, all breeds in fact, but the Scottie has addicts. People who have owned this breed have become devoted to them, and Scotties tend to return such loyalty with an intensity that can make them less than the perfect family dog. They can be one-mannish, but that is not inevitable. They are often feisty, and they like their own turf to themselves, and they do fight. The other man's Scottie who comes bounding up to greet you and lick your hand the first time you meet is rare indeed. More usually, the square, solid, dour little gentleman from the Highlands is reserved. He takes his time and gives his love carefully. But once given, it is yours to keep.

The Highlands of Scotland have produced five Terriers: there is the Scottie, the Dandie Dinmont, the Westy, the handsome Skye (a lovely animal from the Isle of Skye, the Hebrides island closest to the Scottish mainland), and there is also the Cairn, a sweet little animal. Four other Terriers originated in Ireland: the Irish, the Soft-Coated Wheaten, the Norwich, and the splendid Kerry Blue. All of the other Terrier breeds come from England, Wales, and Germany. Clearly, the British island complex is the Terrier capital of the world.

The Scottie is a special dog for special people. He must be respected and not forced to oversocialize. He likes his private people on private ground, and he doesn't like other animals pushing in. He is bright, alert, sure of himself, and a little hard-nosed about life. He is also the idol of a cult.

Airedale Terrier: They call him the king of the Terriers, and indeed he is the largest of the Terrier group. He is also loyal and powerful and fine in many ways.

You will need a crystal ball to trace the Airedale back much beyond the middle of the last century. He is probably down from a breed now extinct, the Old

English or Broken-Haired Terrier, and that breed was probably mixed with a coarse-coated Otter Hound to add swimming ability and a good nose to an already first-rate dog. The breed came to be called Airedale after the Airedale Dog Show in England, where a group of Waterside Terriers, near ancestors of the Airedale, made a particularly good showing.

Most of the good American Airedale lines are descended from one English dog, Champion Clonmel Monarch. Our Airedales run to twenty-three inches, and that is a tall Terrier, with weights to fifty pounds. By nature, the Airedale is bold and courageous, and he can be aggressive. He has been bred as a Working Dog, though, so he isn't as high-strung or hysterical as other Terriers can be. He is easy to train, very loyal, good with kids he knows and loves, and is a superb ratter. He is also a retriever, fine in the water. He is hardy and fast, a very energetic dog that is not for the situation where a sedentary animal is desired. Some people have good luck with Airedales in apartments, but they are so big and so full of beans, I prefer them in the country, or at least in the suburbs. The Airedale, because of his breeding and style, needs exercise, and it is only fair to give the dog what he was bred to have.

The Airedale coat is rich tan with black or grizzle markings. Hard, dense, and quite wiry, it lies close to the body and doesn't need a lot of care, just the occasional brushing.

The Airedale isn't an expensive dog to buy—pet-quality animals can be found for under $150—but neither is it a dog that should be considered for purchase from anyone but a specialty breeder who has really put his or her all into this breed, into loving it and bettering it. Skip the mills, and stick with the people who really love the Airedale.

West Highland White Terrier: They have been known as Roseneath Terriers and Poltalloch Terriers, and James I referred to them as "earth dogs"; we call them the West Highland White Terrier.

The Terriers of Scotland—the Scottie, the Cairn, the Skye, the Dandie Dinmont, and the Westy—all came down from the basic Terrier stock of Scotland, or so it is generally believed today. Of this mixed bag of Highland, none is more endearing than the Westy. Dogs of this breed stand to eleven inches and weigh as much as nineteen pounds. That is all love and action, mind you, all personality and Scots spunk. The coat is white, hard to the touch, and about two inches long without curl.

The typical Westy is brave and tough; he is assertive and demanding of love. He is about a perfect pet for the apartment, the house, the farm, anywhere. True to his Scots tradition, he is not bothered by weather; he is as hardy as they come. He loves to play, for he has to feel that he belongs and can participate in the action, whatever the action might be. Friends of mine have a Westy who goes berserk unless you sit forward in your chair and let him push his nose into your pocket and steal your handkerchief. It is his favorite game. Not all Westies, of course, are thieves like our friend Tiger.

Westies do shed and should be brushed often. They are grand-looking dogs when in good coat, neatly plucked and brushed, and clean. They have a square, positive, and very Scots look about them. Many people wonder what a good apartment dog might be, and this is one answer, the West Highland White Terrier. Their reputation for being one-man dogs is only occasionally borne out by the facts. I find most Westies gregarious and happy to be appreciated by guests. They can be scrappy, though, and, if they are to share a home with cats, must be broken to the idea early. They just love to tree cats. All of life, in fact, is a game to the West Highland White Terrier.

Be careful to buy wisely when you seek an example of the breed. Puppy mills have specialized in mass-producing Westies because their appeal as puppies guarantees sales. Buy only from specialty breeders, only from people who really love this breed and have devoted their lives to it.

Cairn Terrier: They love their native Terriers on the Isle of Skye and in the Western Highlands of Scotland. But they love another breed perhaps as much or even more.

The Cairn Terrier, they say, could be the ancestor of the Scottie, the West Highland White Terrier, and the Skye. It is a breed very much alive today. The smallest of the working Terriers, the Cairn is used on the Isle of Skye to rout out fox, badger, otter, and other creatures considered vermin.

The Cairn runs to fourteen pounds, that is the acceptable size here and in England, with heights to ten inches in the dog and about the same in the bitch, maybe an inch less. Any color but white will do; wheatens and tans are common, as is a kind of grizzled look, but white is not allowed. The coat has a hard feeling and protects the dog from all weather.

The Cairn is a hardy little animal, and when you consider the weather they have off the Atlantic coast of Scotland, you can see why that would be. One of the nice things about the Cairn, and there are a number, is that both American and British breeders have shown determination in maintaining the dog as it was a hundred, two hundred, even three hundred years ago. The Cairn today is as feisty, as much of a personality, as much all-dog, as it probably ever was. It makes an outstanding pet, although it can be one-mannish. The breed is cautious with strangers, it doesn't like crowds, and it can be jealous. But it can also adapt to any kind of life, and it will make out just fine in an apartment. Cairns are lively and loyal and quite clean. They shed very little as Terriers go, and although they like to run and work the countryside, they don't need all that much exercise. They can compete with children in a family, but are, perhaps, better off living with one or two people who want to treat them as children. They are ferociously devoted in such circumstances. I don't think they are necessarily the best mixers, and probably they are better off where there are no other household pets. They do vary, not all Cairns are the same by any means, but that is the generalized picture.

Fox Terrier: He is one of the best-known purebred dogs in the world, popular everywhere dogs are appreciated.

There are two kinds of Fox Terrier, the Smooth and the Wirehaired. They used to be interbred regularly, but not in recent years. The Smooth was the first of the two to be recognized in the show ring, although the Wirehaired is probably an older form. The Smooth came into being around 1790, by which time the Wirehaired had been used on fox for decades. In fact, the breed was originally shown as a Sporting Dog, not a Terrier. The ancestors of the Smooth Fox Terrier were probably the Beagle, the Greyhound, and the smooth-coated Black-and-Tan Terrier of old England. The ancestry of the Wirehaired Fox Terrier almost certainly included the rough working Terriers of Wales, Derbyshire, and Durham.

The Fox Terrier today stands to fifteen and a half

inches in the dog, an inch less in the bitch, and weights run from sixteen to eighteen pounds. The Smooth, of course, has a smooth, flat, hard coat. It should be abundant. The Fox in the Wirehaired form should have a hard and wiry coat. The basic color is white, with markings of black and tan.

The overall impression the Fox Terrier gives is one of readiness—for anything. Feisty, at times hyperactive, willing, bright, assertive, badly in need of good training and constant control, a lover but possibly one-mannish, this is a breed for the fun-loving, dog-loving individual willing to make a commitment to play. The Fox Terrier hates being bored. It wants fun and games for hours every day and should be kept in a reasonably active situation where there will be at least a chance to burn off some steam. It makes a great suburban dog, is fine on a farm, and perfectly OK in an apartment, as long as its active nature is provided for. A fine watchdog, it will bark at anything.

Leash laws should always be observed, because the Fox Terrier can lose his cool and take off after another dog, a cat, or some kids running by. You can't always depend on him to come when he is called, especially if he is excited, unless you have really worked at training him. An awful lot of Fox Terriers get hit by cars because of their dash-first-think-later attitude toward life.

A great dog for the right people, but a first-class pain in the wagging tail for the person not totally committed to a hairy perpetual-motion machine; that is the Fox Terrier in any hairstyle.

THE TOY BREEDS

Pekingese: Stealing an example of this breed in ancient China was worse than stealing a horse in the American

West. Out West they just hung you, in China the Pekingese thief was tortured to death.

The little lion dog, the little sun dog, the dog behind the Foo dog . . . the Pekingese became known to the Western world in 1860 when the British, Lord love them, sacked the imperial palace in Peking. Most of the Chinese in the palace killed their sacred dogs rather than allow them to fall into the hands of the beak-noses. But apparently, the aunt of the emperor couldn't bring herself to destroy her beloved pets—she committed suicide, leaving her four dogs behind some drapery. They were discovered and carried off to England. One went to Queen Victoria, and the other three were used for breeding. The Pekingese became, within thirty-odd years, immensely popular, and there the matter stands today.

The Pekingese dog can stand to nine inches and weigh as much as ten pounds, but smaller specimens are more common. The long, straight coat can be red, fawn, black, tan, sable, or brindle, or any combination. The face has a black mask. The spirit of this dog is legendary. It is afraid of nothing, will back away from nothing. It barks readily and is a good watchdog. It is hardy, tough, and very regal; proud as a peacock, to coin a phrase.

The Pekingese is a near-perfect apartment dog. A short walk a couple of times a day will see to its exercise needs, and a lot of loving, an awful lot of loving, is in order. In Imperial China, eunuchs were assigned to care for the royal dogs, and slave girls were used as wet nurses to raise them after their own human babies had been put to death to save the milk for the dogs. That sort of thing is generally out of order now, but the Pekingese acts as if he hadn't heard.

This is a dog that wants to play, wants attention, wants to be included in everything. It can be, but need not necessarily be, a slow friend when it comes to strangers. Loyalty is often confined to immediate family. Pekingese can be aggressive little joys, and it is moot whether they are good family dogs with children around. Some owners find they are; others find they are not. They *are* super in a home with people of advanced age who can take pleasure watching the imperious little rascal carrying on and running the show. He does need brushing every day, but that is no great problem with so small a mote.

When you think Pekingese, think professional breeder only.

Yorkshire Terrier: They make bigger dogs and fatter dogs, there are faster dogs and skinnier dogs, and some have longer tails and shorter hair, but in all this world there is no spunkier, doggier dog than the Yorkshire Terrier.

The Yorkie comes from England. He isn't a very old breed, but his popularity has continued to grow until today he is close to being a fad. Dark steel blue or silver blue and tan, the Yorkshire Terrier is a dream of an apartment dog. He is one of the most pleasant of all the Toys. He may weigh as little as two and a half pounds or go to seven or eight pounds. The smaller specimens are usually more expensive.

No one knows what the ancestry of this breed might have been. There are theories that bring in Skye Terriers, Black-and-Tan Terriers, Maltese, and even Dandie Dinmonts, and it is likely that from within that group the Yorkshire bloodline began. In the century or so since they came into being, the Yorkies have been refined until a dream has been realized: with the modern world overstuffed as it is, the Yorkie has become the perfect city canine. He is tougher than most people think and can take it when he has to. Yorkies make good watchdogs, though they don't like being left alone. They were designed as a dog you take along. I have seen many a Yorkie in a pocketbook, and although you might like something a little more manly yourself, so portable a dog can fill a very important need.

Yorkies don't shed very much, and they get along with other animals and people. They should be brushed often if they are to keep that silken look, and if you like ribbons in dogs' hair, the Yorkie will usually tolerate one. (Personally, I like my dogs nude.) This is not an inexpensive breed, and $150 will only get you started.

Do Yorkies get along with children? Decidedly yes, better than some other Toys I can think of, by a wide margin. Because they are so intelligent and responsive and basically good-natured, they are an excellent breed for the youngster who wants to try an amateur's hand at showing. A great first breed for the new showman.

A word of warning: the Yorkshire Terrier is exceedingly fast on its feet. I have had two friends who failed to see their Yorkie leap to get into the car with them. In both cases, the dogs were caught in slamming car doors. One was killed and the other was severely injured. So watch your speedy little Yorkie, it could break your heart by getting into trouble you never thought existed.

Chihuahua: He is probably the smallest dog in the world, and he is extremely popular. The Chihuahua is named for the Mexican state of Chihuahua; this is a bit misleading, for the breed originated in Asia, it is believed, and may have been crossed with a small Mexican dog along the way. Today, most come from the United States, not Mexico.

The Chihuahua can weigh anywhere from one to six pounds, although two to four is a healthier spread. Dogs and bitches are the same size, up to five inches tall. Colors can be anything, solid or marked, and in any combination. The coat is smooth and glossy in the smooth-coated variety and soft and curly in the long-coated, rarer (in the US) variety.

This is a breed that need never be taken out. A Chihuahua is not sociable with other animals, generally: all he wants is his family close by where he can order them around. He should not be exposed to cold weather and is prone to rheumatism. He is a clean little dog, he doesn't shed, and he is extremely loyal to his master. He does not take to strangers and will bite. He doesn't belong in a family with children, although there are exceptions to that. He is better off with a limited family, older people particularly, who will baby him and answer his every whim.

He is a picky eater and fussy about his rights and privileges. He is perfect for a shut-in or a family that cannot provide exercise and outside action, which he neither needs nor wants. All of these points are generalizations, of course, and there will always be the exceptional dog that will be different on every count. Generally, though, this is the perfect apartment dog for the home without small children. He isn't as fragile as he looks (he couldn't be and survive), but he can't take roughhousing with a youngster either. He can get his pencil-thin legs injured. The Chihuahua will bark on the approach of strangers, and that can be comforting. He is exceedingly loyal with one or two people and not very keen on more than that in his life. He can be fun, and he is to spoil. That is what he was designed for.

Beware of buying Chihuahuas from pet shops. This breed requires careful breeding, and the only example you should consider is one you can discuss with the people who brought it into the world. Pay them a visit, and see the adults in their line.

Pomeranian: Would you believe that a five-pound dog was descended from the sled dogs of Iceland and Lapland? Not only that, in the last century it weighed thirty pounds and was used for herding sheep in England. Now he is more for the silk cushion and the bonbon set. I refer to Mr. Personality himself, the Pomeranian.

The Pomeranian (so called because much of the breeding down to present Toy size was done in Pomerania) is one of the group known as the Spitz dogs. In this country, the Spitz isn't a breed, but a subgroup, and that is where the unknown roots of Pomeranian stock lie.

Today's Pomeranian weighs between three and seven pounds and stands no more than seven inches at the shoulder. The coat is long, straight, and it gleams and glistens like freshly minted coins. Colors are all over the lot: black, brown, beaver, red, chocolate, orange, blue, white, cream, and something called wolf-sable. The Pomeranian can be solid or parti-colored and variously marked. The important thing with this breed is spirit. This is a dog with style and class, with fire inside. He is proud, and he prances as well as bounces. He is sure and assertive and not always the best creature around other pets. He is loyal, but he is also jealous and possessive. Generally, I do not like this dog. I have known exceptions, but in the main, they aren't all that keen on being handled by kids for they are, after all, kids themselves. With children, they can be snappy, and although a bite from a Pomeranian will not result in a traumatic wound, it can draw tears.

The Pomeranian is for someone who wants a baby that will remain a baby, a spirited, fiery baby, but a perennial child nonetheless. For such people, it can be the perfect companion, pretty and loaded with high style and personality. The Pomeranian is also a watchdog, friend, and confidante. In fact, I think it just might be true that the pretty little Pomeranian is the largest dog in the world all tucked into a tiny body.

Shih Tzu: In 1969 a new breed of dog was admitted to the list of the American Kennel Club, a new breed to our shores, at least. The breed was actually an ancient one from China, a chrysanthemum-faced dog (so regarded because of the way the hair grows around the face) known as the Shih Tzu, which means, in Chinese, "the lion." There is an old Buddhist belief, or at least saying, that there was once an association between the deity and the lion, and somehow that association resulted in this lovely little canine.

No one really knows how the Shih Tzu reached China. It was an awfully long time ago, for objects of art depicting this breed go back to the seventeenth century. Some stories have him coming from the fabled Hidden Valleys of Tibet, others say that he was tribute paid to the Chinese emperors by the Byzantine Empire. We will never know. What we do know is that this affectionate little beauty of a Toy was raised in the court by eunuchs who tried to outdo each other in the quality of the dogs they produced. Those responsible for dogs the emperor took a fancy to were rewarded well. I guess if they made you a eunuch just to have you work in a kennel, you deserved some goodies now and then.

Shih Tzus, all legends and exotic tales aside, make sensational pets. They run to ten inches or so and

should not weigh more than fifteen pounds. Often they
are much less than that. The coat is luxurious, that is
the appropriate word. Long and dense, it can be wavy,
at least slightly so in some examples, but it must not be
curly. There is a good woolly undercoat. All colors are
allowed. And the movement? Well, it is a kind of
smooth flow with a slight roll to it. There is a good drive
from the rear end, and overall, the little beast has a
proud demeanor.

This is an active, alert little animal, smart and proud
and loving. Kept in good shape, it is a thing of beauty,
and its popularity is bound to continue the increase it
has shown in recent years. Beware of spare-time breeders on this one, only the specialist will do when you
think Shih Tzu.

Pug: He is a Toy for sure, in size, style, and personality. A barrel-shaped little dog, the Pug was born to be
spoiled, and if you don't spoil him you might ruin him.

A very long time ago, traders working for the Dutch
East India Company returned to Europe with a small
dog from China. It was an immediate success with the
ladies of high style, and still is. Like a great many
breeds from Asia, and especially from China, the Pug
has a short nose, a large head, and a tail curled high
and over the rump. It is actually a terrible design for a
dog, but the Pug has made it through to what is apparently eternal popularity.

Pugs aren't very large, only ten or eleven inches at
the shoulder and up to perhaps eighteen pounds. The
color is all black, or silver to fawn with a black face
and some black on the tail. The coat is smooth and
glossy, and tends to be soft and fine. No one should
dream of owning a Pug unless he is really daffy about
dogs, because this is one breed in constant need of love

and approval. It wants to be with you at all times, it wants to sleep on your bed, it wants to play tug-of-war and fetch. It loves toys, it loves people, and it is born spoiled rotten. Although small and rather placid, it has stamina and courage. It isn't a fussy breed. It eats well and really isn't all that temperamental, although a Pug can be jealous of another dog.

Pugs don't smell badly outside, but like all short-nosed dogs, they are air gulpers, and that fact expresses itself, usually when you have a room full of guests, in a very distinctive way. Pugs don't drool the way Bulldogs do, and that is certainly in their favor. They are stubborn dogs and will take training or not as they see fit. That can be exasperating.

I would avoid Pugs when there are very small children, but as the kids begin to grow and approach school age, this is a good breed for the apartment. As a matter of fact, I can't think of a better apartment dog, all other things being equal.

This much is certain: if you are a Pug fan, nothing will make you waver in your affection. I know people who really couldn't live without a Pug or two around (they are often owned in pairs or braces). A nice little dog for a junior showman to start out with, because the grooming is minimal, the Pug is a smart little dog, too, and in this case that means both intelligent and stylish.

Maltese: They call him a Terrier, although he is in fact a Spaniel. He is shown as a Toy. When Malta was thought by many to be the center of the cultural universe (fifteen hundred years before Christ), this dog was the center of the universe on Malta.

The Maltese is the darling of history and refinement.

Under seven pounds, smaller if possible, down to four pounds desired, pure white, silky, and all fun, that is what the standards call for. As far back as 3500 B.C., they spoke of this dog. The Apostle Paul did, and later Publius, the Roman governor of Malta, wrote of the breed (and had one he called Issa); Callimachus the Elder, who died in 322 B.C., Strabo, Pliny the Elder, Saint Clement, all recorded this dog for history, and many of them owned and loved the breed.

For all of these thousands of years, the refined cultures of the Mediterranean toasted this precious little canine. At the time of Queen Elizabeth I, a specimen sold for the equivalent of $2,000. That would be in the high five figures today. Linnaeus wrote of them, and so have nature writers up to the present day. What's so special?

The Maltese is one of the best natured of all the tiny dogs, one of the prettiest, one of the brightest and hardiest, and one of the most delightful. Women adore Maltese, children get along with them just fine. They are perfect in the apartment, in the shopping bag, in the purse. This is the kind of dog you take along and nobody need know, unless you want to make a point of letting them know.

Clean, adoring as a companion, and easy to adore, a Maltese is the dream dog for people who want this kind of pet. Once upon a time, queens fed their Maltese from golden pitchers, giving them only the rarest and most treasured delicacies. That isn't really necessary, though; your Maltese will eat dog food. Gold dishes and slaves to serve them are optional, of course. The characteristic is what I call *neotony*, the retention of juvenile traits. That is what a lot of people want in a dog, and that is what they get in a Maltese. Buy from the specialty breeder only, for this is a special breed.

Silky Terrier: The Silky Terrier was not recognized as a breed in this country until 1959, when it was admitted to registry by the American Kennel Club. It was apparently a cross between the tough little Australian Terrier and the Yorkshire. Although undoubtedly developed as a pet, it has done its fair share of work on Australian poultry farms where it handles the rat situation and, they say, snakes. Knowing a little about Australian snakes, I find that somewhat hard to believe, but there you have it, the claim.

Today's Silky Terrier is shown in the Toy class, although it is Terrier in disposition and talent. Dogs run to ten inches and ten pounds, bitches only slightly less. The coat is fine and glossy, silky as the name implies, and it lies flat to the body. The color combination is standard black-and-tan, although the black is more often really a blue, one of several blues running from silver to slate.

The Silky is a character, let's establish that, a kind of superdog pushed down into a tiny body. It is clean, doesn't shed much, and is easy to maintain. A few minutes of brushing is all that is needed to keep the coat lovely. It is an almost ideal apartment dog. It is small enough to pick up and carry anywhere in a carrier, handbag, or in your arms. It is a good little watchdog—that's the Terrier showing through despite the Toy status. It loves to be admired and wants to participate. This is one of those breeds that never really grows up and would be perfect for people who want a baby around to fuss over and be fussed over by.

There are some pretty poor Silkies around, examples that look like crosses between a badger and a cockroach (a difficult genetic feat to accomplish). I would stay close to the specialty breeder with this one. There are a lot of casual or incidental breeders around, but they are not for the kind of Silky Terrier you want. If you have limited space, but want a dog at least as big inside as an Irish Wolfhound, think of the ten-inch, ten-pound Silky Terrier, the superdog from Australia.

THE NON-SPORTING BREEDS

Poodles: Don't let the haircut fool you. You can't tell a dog by the way he wears his hair any more than you can a man.

Because of his many fancy hairdos and the attention often paid him by little old ladies, some people tend to think of the Poodle as a sissy, strictly a lady's dog. They just couldn't be more wrong. There is probably no other dog in the world that has been as popular for so long, or so often represented in art and literature. No one is sure where he came from originally, but the name "*French* Poodle" is new and misleading. He was in Germany before he was in France, and the German word *pudelin,* meaning "to splash in water," is undoubtedly where his English name stems from. I read someplace that the breed may have originated in Russia and that Gypsies were peddling the Poodle on their travels across Europe nine hundred years ago, but I wouldn't offer that as a fact. Wherever he came from, he was a water dog. He is a fantastic swimmer and, it is believed, was once a retriever. Originally, those funny haircuts were designed to help the animal swim, since the Poodle's coat grows more rapidly than that of any other breed of dog. One especially nice thing about him, in fact, is that he doesn't shed.

There are three different Poodles, or at least three different sizes. (They actually all are the same breed.) The Standard is over fifteen inches tall; the Miniature is fifteen inches or under, but not under ten; and the Toy is under ten inches. A Standard dog can weigh almost sixty pounds, and a Toy bitch as little as five. Poodles are supposed to be solid in color and have no markings. They can be black, brown, white, blue, apricot, silver, or creamy coffee. Those other colors you see, ones like lavender and shocking pink, are dyes, applied to match some lady's outfit or sitting-room decor. I don't suppose it hurts the dog, but I think it's silly and just a little weird. That's only one man's opinion, however.

Certainly one characteristic of the breed is intelligence. Many experts believe the Poodle to be the most intelligent of all dogs, and I tend to agree, having owned two myself. Poodles are playful, alert, affectionate, and can be trained easily. I don't happen to like performing animals—not in homes, on television, or in circuses—but Poodles apparently can be taught to do just about anything but read. They are quick and eager, and generally quite pleasant. A good Poodle, in any size or color, is not an inexpensive animal to buy. While its popularity has inspired some mass-production techniques based on excessive inbreeding, which has resulted in some pretty dreadful-looking dogs, serious breeders have maintained a standard of excellence worthy of the breed. You can get a pretty nice-looking Poodle of pet quality for about $150 rock bottom. If you are thinking of show quality, think more about $1,000. And they do have to be clipped, or they look like a pile of rags.

The Poodle is a dog for the more-intense-than-average dog lover. It is a lot of dog, with a great deal of potential for learning and companionship. There is a world of difference, I find, between the Standard (or Giant, as some people call it) and the Toy. The latter may or may not be the best dog for children. I have seen it both ways. More often than not, though, a dog reflects his home life. A nervous dog often comes from a home where hysteria is not uncommon. Before buying your Poodle, consider which size suits your way of life and what end of the scale you want to buy in at: pet or show dog.

Lhasa Apso: He comes from Tibet, where his name (approximately *Abso Seng Kye*) translates as "Bark Lion Sentinel Dog" or "Bark Sentinel Lion Dog."

For over eight hundred years, the Lhasa Apso was the darling of Tibetan royalty. Specimens of this coveted breed were favorite gifts from the Dalai Lama to visiting dignitaries, and centuries ago, many were presented to the royal household of China. It is one of the four breeds to come to us from Tibet. There are also the Tibetan Terrier, the lovely little Tibetan Spaniel, and the powerful Tibetan Mastiff. The Mastiff was the guard dog, and the Lhasa Apso worked inside, giving and getting love. It was bred to be spoiled, so if that is what you seek in a dog, this could be your breed. All enchantment and love, he is naturally the center of attraction.

If you like history, you might be interested to know that the first two examples of this breed to arrive on American shores were named Taikoo and Dinkie. Dinkie was the color of raw silk, and Taikoo was mixed black and white.

The Lhasa Apso isn't a very large dog, about eleven inches at the shoulder and up to fifteen pounds. The coat is heavy and straight as befits a mountain dog. It should be neither woolly nor silky. The breed does require care—a lot of brushing and combing if it is to look its regal best. Breeders in Tibet apparently didn't prefer any particular color, and almost anything goes

—gold, white, black, brown, and parti-color. Since the Lhasa Apso is so much a child itself, there is some question as to how good it is around children, but the folks I know who have owned this breed have found it a lovely family dog as long as it gets plenty of attention. It is demanding, and it is also bright, responsive, and easily trained by a determined, gentle owner. The eyes of the Lhasa Apso are attentive and alert. Watch them the next time you see one of these dogs.

This is a very special breed of dog for people with time and love to offer. The Retriever was bred to retrieve, the Doberman to guard, and the Lhasa Apso to love. Pick the dog that is right for you.

Boston Terrier: He is one of the few true native American breeds, the gentle Non-Sporting Dog from Boston. The Boston Terrier, up to seventeen inches high and weighing no more than twenty-five pounds, was obtained by crossing the English Bulldog and the White English Terrier. Following that initial cross, there was a lot of inbreeding, all this in the years following the Civil War. The Boston Terrier Club was established in 1891, but real progress in standards and quality came after the turn of the century.

This kind, affectionate, gentle little dog is still one of the most popular in America, although nowhere near as popular as he was thirty years ago. He is eminently trainable and reacts to the people around him in an almost supernatural way. He seems to feel moods and interact with them. He is a fine little guard dog without being excessively yappy. He is just about the perfect apartment dog—doesn't shed too much and doesn't require much space.

Like all dogs, the Boston does like his exercise, and although he will adjust to almost anything, including sharing the life of a shut-in, it is nice to see that he gets some outside exercise whenever possible. Very few dogs love toys the way this breed does, and a Boston goes fairly mad at the sight of a ball. He will retrieve one by the hour, in or out of doors. In fact, a Boston that has been allowed to play with a rubber ball will drive you crazy unless you throw it for him. Expect the ball at your feet every time you try to move, and expect those eyes, those big, expressive eyes, begging for your participation in a game of toss and fetch. Go ahead, try to ignore them. Does the breed have faults? Indeed! Like short-nosed dogs everywhere, Bostons tend to gulp air and can be gassy. They also snore and snort (it makes them sound very uncomfortable and contented), and they do vomit when they get too excited. The coat, of course, is short and smooth; the texture is fine; colors are either brindle or black with white markings. They should have a healthy sheen to their coats. They should be alert, active, willing, and never cranky.

A good breed, the Boston, one America can be proud to have developed.

Dalmatian: Some say he originated in Europe, some say Africa, some say Asia. No one really knows. He is one of the most ancient of breeds, one of the most distinguishable, the dog the British call the Plum Pudding Dog and we call the Dalmatian. The Gypsies loved these dogs and took them back and forth across the world. The breed we know was first recognized in Dalmatia, the former Austrian province on the eastern shore of the Adriatic. There is no reason to think the breed originated there, however; the name is a convenience, it does not identify origin.

The Dalmatian is white with black or dark brown spots. The puppies are born white and their markings develop as they grow. The breed stands to twenty-three inches at the withers and weighs as much as fifty pounds. If you want to know what the Dalmatian has done through history, just make a list of all the ways dogs can be used: war dog, sentinel, draft dog, shepherd, ratter, watchdog, circus performer, field dog, retriever. He is so good-natured, so willing, so smart that he can learn anything. He is the one and only recognized, official coach dog. He can run with a coach and never get stepped on or run over. He loves horses, and horses seem to like Dalmatians. He is loyal and loving to his family, and in time, learns to accept outsiders. He is not aggressive, is fine with all other animals, doesn't harm livestock, doesn't fight, likes cats, and loves games and exercise. His coat is short, hard, and glossy, and he is neat, clean, and rugged.

Don't even go look at Dalmatian puppies to see *if* you want one. That is hopeless, for as puppies they are irresistible. It would take an ironhearted soul not to succumb, instantly. By the way, there is an occasional inherited fault. Beware of deafness when you start looking for puppies. This is a super dog for the house, questionable for the apartment. And watch the feeding. A Dalmatian will run to fat if you are not careful.

By all means, visit a specialty breeder, and consider this ancient aristocrat among breeds, he who followed the chariots of Rome even as he does the fire engine today, that English coaching dog from Austria and beyond.

Keeshond: It isn't very often that the history of a dog is written in terms of political events, but there is a dog that was a symbol of people during a time of great unrest. I refer to the national dog of Holland, the Keeshond.

In the late 1700s Europe was in a state of potentially violent upheaval. The French Revolution was brewing, and Holland, too, felt the surge and the thrust of the time. In Holland, two parties formed into opposing camps; there were the followers of the Prince of Orange, called the partisans or *prinsgezinden,* and there were the patriots or *patriotten.* The latter were generally middle-class people, and they were led by a man named Kees De Gyselaer of Dordrecht. He was a dog lover, and he owned a little dog called Kees. It was from that dog the name Keeshond came. The *patriotten* needed a symbol, and the small dog Kees represented was so much a part of the Dutch scene (the breed had been known in Holland for centuries) that Kees was it. The fact that he became the symbol of a whole Dutch political movement is not surprising, for the Dutch have traditionally been dog lovers. As fate would have it, the cause of the Prince of Orange prevailed, and people who owned Keeshonden (that is the plural form) got rid of them for fear of being discriminated against as owners of living symbols of a lost cause. It wasn't until the 1920s that the Baroness Van Hardenbroek decided to try to salvage the breed. She found many more excellent examples than she ever imagined existed, tucked away here and there in corners of Holland. So the Keeshond made its comeback.

This quiet, sensible companion dog is Spitz-like in appearance and is a pleasing mixture of gray and black. The coat is long, and the tail is a lovely plume. Males stand to eighteen inches, bitches to seventeen. Characteristically, there are spectacles, delicately penciled lines slanting upward from the outer corners of the eyes to the lower corners of the ears.

Keeshonden are affectionate, reliable homebodies, fine with kids, fine with the elderly, not hunters, not snappy, and always ready to give and get a measure of love. They do require brushing, but not much exercise. This is a fine breed, too little known and appreciated in this country, with a history that is full of intrigue and adventure. It is probably the ancestral breed of the Pomeranian.

Chow Chow: The Polar Bear has a blue-black tongue and so does one breed of dog, the Chow Chow—a fact that has actually raised the suggestion that the Polar Bear and the Chow Chow are related (they are about as much so as the Chihuahua and the Grizzly Bear).

The Chow Chow comes from China and is exceedingly ancient—well over two thousand years old and perhaps older than that, we don't know. The Chinese emperors had a nasty habit (they had lots of nasty habits) of obliterating their forebears' culture, so the record of this dog's origin is lost in the dust of time. The name Chow Chow does not come from pickles or eating habits. The old China traders used to load up with loot of all kinds, carved ivory, porcelain, and other works of art. They used a Chinese word for bric-a-brac, *chow chow*, and listed all their wares by that name. They used to bring in some dogs, too, and undoubtedly that is how the dog came to be called by that name. That is not its name in China.

The splendid Chow Chow was originally a hunting and working dog, and the emperors maintained vast kennels with thousands of the breed. Our Chow Chow today stands to twenty inches and can weigh sixty pounds. The dense, long, straight coat can be red, fawn, black, or blue. The dog should be heavy-looking and square. The sense one gets is of power. The Chow Chow today is shown as a Non-Sporting breed, and its use in the field in this part of the world is a vestige of its past (though it is said to be still used on pheasant in some parts of Asia).

This is a one-man dog that can be distrustful of strangers to a degree that may be troublesome. It is an undemonstrative breed, and I for one have never seen a Chow Chow look particularly happy about anything. But don't let that dour expression fool you. A Chow Chow with his master, secure in the relationship, is apparently a very happy dog. I do not trust this breed around children, although that is not to say it wouldn't be good with the kids in its own family. But kids attract kids, and what about the new kid on the block who comes by for a tussle? There are exceptions, certainly, and I am sure there have been living dolls among the Chow Chow ranks. It is just that I see it as a special breed of great power and beauty for the special home situation. It needs careful training and absolute control by a masterful master.

Schipperke: A very interesting dog is the small Non-Sporting breed, the Schipperke, or Shipperke, as some people spell it. The correct pronounciation is *skee-er-ker*. The name comes from the Flemish and means "little captain." The breed comes from the Flemish provinces of Belgium, not Holland, as is sometimes claimed. They were actually bred down in size from a kind of Belgian Sheepdog. The same Sheepdog bred up became a breed known in this country, the Groenendael.

Although the Schipperke is superficially Spitz-like, it is not a Spitz breed. It is always solid black, and the coat is full and slightly harsh to the touch. Shoulder height in the male is up to thirteen inches and the weight should not be over eighteen pounds. It is not true that this breed is characteristically born tailless. The tail is docked, and the standards call for the maximum remaining length to be no more than one inch. Schipperkes are sometimes referred to as barge dogs, and indeed, some were kept on barges and boats as watchdogs. They didn't attack the intruder, or even bark at him; rather they paddled softly from barge to barge along the pier and got their owner to come see to the matter.

This is a fine small apartment dog, a fine pet for children, a good all-around family dog. Schipperkes like attention, they like to play, they are watchdogs, and they need exercise. This breed does shed, so a fair brushing will help keep dog and home neat and tidy. There is really no other breed that looks at all like the compact little Schipperke, and when you see one with that ruff and full coat, that tailless silhouette, you will know what you are seeing. A ratter, a friend, a kid's pal, a guarder of your castle, think about that unusual dog, the Schipperke, and when you do think only of specialty breeders. This is a breed that must not be mass-produced, or we will end up with a raunchy-looking, nondescript, Terrier-like dog.

4
CATS

Man and the Cat: The great Napoleon: leader of armies, conqueror of the world, strategic genius who feared nothing? Not exactly true. The great emperor broke into a cold sweat if a kitten walked into the room. He was afraid of cats.

It works both ways. Men and women have adored their cats as well as hated them. When Queen Victoria died, her favorite, a white cat named White Heather, was kept under the protection of the royal family and died many years later, to the grief of King Edward VII. Hemingway loved cats and kept one around when he worked, and the same was true of Cardinal Richelieu. Yet, the Duc de Noailles was so thoroughly terrified of cats that when Louis XV walked up behind him and *meowed*, the duke fell to the floor in a dead faint.

Men and women have worshiped cats, adored them, despised them, left them fortunes, burned them alive, and laid awake at night thinking up new tortures for them. Cats have been characterized as the bringers of good and the harbingers of evil. Their actions have been studied in order to foretell the future, and they have been thought to have the power to cure any illness. Thomas Wolsey held a cat in his arms throughout his working day. Sir Walter Scott liked to have a cat playing around him while he worked. Lord Roberts, the British field marshal who defeated the Boers in South Africa, would break into a sweat and swear he couldn't breathe at the sight of a cat (perhaps he was in fact allergic). Pope Leo XIII had Micetto, a little mongrel cat born somewhere in the Vatican. He was raised by the pope and lay about in the folds of the pontiff's robes. Other great fans of cats have been Louis Pasteur, Albert Einstein, and Albert Schweitzer. Samuel Johnson worshiped cats, they say, as did Victor Hugo.

So it has been throughout known history: devil and saint, object of adoration, and target of abuse. Man has been, in both directions, absolutely neurotic when it comes to cats. Why has this enormous range of emotional fervor not extended to our relationship with dogs? I don't know. We are rational about dogs, irrational about cats. It is one of the mysteries of the creature we are, and of the creatures they are. And it is one of the reasons that owning a cat is such a pleasure. It is part of something bigger than ourselves.

Personality of the Cat: The cat came into our circle of life thousands of years ago. No one really knows where, and no one knows when. We do not know the original animal by its rightful name, but somehow, somewhere, man and animal came together. We could not ride the cat like a horse, it did not pull our things in labor or on treks like the ass. It did not drive off the leopard or run down the gazelle, as did the dog, and it was never destined to herd our goats. It couldn't even warn us of intrusion at the mouth of the cave. The keeping of the cat was one of our earliest acts of art. We kept the cat for beauty, and because somehow it said something about life and living. True, it moused and ratted and tidied things a bit, but that was later when there were barns and houses. The cat came long before that. We kept the cat because of the feel of its fur and the look of its eye; its form pleased us, as did its demeanor. It didn't grovel. It stood and looked at man and dared him to be good and wise. The personality of the cat has always amazed us, so much so that we have wanted and kept the cat around for all these millennia of love and mystery.

When men were quite mad and spoke seriously of the devil, the cat was burned alive and otherwise tortured, for such madmen believed that an animal so self-contained, so sure, and above the lowly life of man's nasty walled cities must be the devil or the familiar that guided the Lord of Darkness. But the cat survived, for its personality required that it survive. I think one of the things that has intrigued us about the cat is its timelessness. It came before us, and it will be here after us. We are an episode in its life, just as its life on earth seems to be an episode in some larger continuum. The cat amuses us, it pleases our senses. We like its sound of purr and purpose. But more than that, the cat interests us as an intellectual challenge. It taunts us to believe, to dare to hope that it will love us back. That really is it, I think: for thousands and thousands of years, man has been waiting and hoping that one day he could be certain the cat loves him, too.

A Kitten in the Home: With the cost of living going up and up and up, isn't it grand that the most essential ingredient of all is free? Love! All you have to do to get it is give it. Take, for example, a kitten in the life of a child.

Poems have been written about the relationship between a child and his or her pet. People have painted it, sculpted it, done books on the subject; psychiatrists are even studying it. It goes back to the beginnings of man himself and has its roots in the need of children to have something of their own to love. Kittens are nice to touch, there is tactile pleasure. They are reassuring because they are always there. They are fun to watch and fun to do things with. They don't make demands, don't reject, and don't punish. They offer a love that is highly dependable and not reflective of forces outside.

A cat can be retreated to. It is a point in time, a figure in the cosmos that stands still and waits for you when all else spins furiously on. Children need that. Pets can help when we move, for we take them with us and they help allay the fear of strange places. They help when we lose people by restoring a sense of stability and reality. The rest of the world can seem unreal, a pet kitten or cat cannot.

I have known a lot of pet-starved children and have, in fact, come close to making enemies of their parents, who often happen to be friends or neighbors. When I get the "I-can't-be-bothered" answer, I can pretty well guess I am looking at parents that may have problems ahead. There can be something revealing in a parent who can't be bothered to let his or her child have a pet.

One of the nicest things about a kitten is that it is free, generally. Certainly, you can spend several hundred dollars getting an Abyssinian, a Russian Blue, or one of the fancier Burmese and Siamese show cats, but anyone who wants to can get just as lovable a creature free, with a stop at any pound or humane shelter, perhaps leaving a token payment to help the shelter continue its work. Most of the cats and kittens now available will never be adopted. There just aren't enough homes, although more than a third of the homes in the United States have cats as part of the family.

For many people, Christmas still retains its religious meaning—a soft and gentle time, not just a lot of commercial ballyhoo. Why not give a life at Christmas? What a wonderful time to open up hearts and homes for many of these waifs! You can adopt a kitten, a bringer of joy for fifteen years at least, if you are careful, and you spend almost no money doing it. Can you think of any other gift—a tie, sweater, toy, or game— that will stay intact and in style for fifteen years? And a kitten is a gift that will grow more precious with each passing year. It is a gift that is rewarding every day of its existence.

If you do plan to adopt a kitten, other people in the family can give appropriate gifts of support: a catnip mouse, or a special cushion, a breakaway safety collar, a spaying certificate (or male-altering gift certificate) from a local veterinarian, food, all the things that will make the kitten so special. Perfect for children, but also great for shut-ins and more elderly people. Don't get cute, by the way—don't package the kitten under the tree and frighten it half to death. Find a quieter, more humane way to introduce it into the family on Christmas Eve or morn. And be sure it has had all its shots, that it is healthy and ready to go right to work at the job of trading love.

American Domestic Shorthair: The cat we call the American Domestic Shorthair is probably close to what the earliest domesticated cat looked like in its tabby coat. Cats are not as genetically responsive as are dogs, and that is why the range of styles among dogs is very much greater. Although all domestic cats belong to one species and all domestic dogs to another, there is nothing in catdom that reflects the range, let us say, between a Chihuahua and a Great Dane, or a Papillon and a Great Pyrenees. But there are variations enough. Take that Domestic Shorthair. It comes in a splendid variety of colors: pure white with either blue or orange eyes; dense coal-black with copper or orange eyes; a number of red shades; cream colored; Chinchilla with a pure white undercoat and the hair tipped with black (the effect is silver); and a shaded silver which is unmarked, with eyes usually green or blue-green. The Smoke Shorthair appears black with a white undercoat, and with a silver frill and ear tufts. There is the Brown

Tabby that runs all the way to brilliant coppery brown with dense black markings. There is the handsome Silver Tabby, too, and the Blue Tabby as well; and the Red Tabby can be extremely handsome. Among the most spectacular Shorthairs are the Tortoiseshell, in black, orange, and cream; the Calico, in black, red, and cream; and the Blue Cream.

The Domestic Shorthair cat may not vary all that much in size, in general conformation, or in bizarre styling, but there is enough beautiful and interesting color variation to make the breeding program an art and a carefully controlled science.

All of these color varieties can be found in almost any pound or humane animal shelter, and a few trips will be sure to turn up just the one you are looking for. No one, in the name of art or science, should be breeding anything but the most exquisite show cats, and then only to perpetuate a line. A great deal of soul-searching should precede anyone's producing another litter of kittens in this country, since millions must be destroyed annually for the want of a good home.

Short-haired White Cat: There are varieties of cats in America today often referred to as British Shorthairs; this is to distinguish them from the more exotic foreign cats like the Siamese and the Burmese.

Let's consider the all-white British Shorthair. All British varieties are generally calm and pleasant animals with open, willing faces, and so it is with the British White. Its coat seems almost translucent and should be pure white without marking or tone. There is a blue-eyed variety and another with orange eyes. Sometimes, the blue-eyes, a difficult line to improve, are too pale, and these cats are often stone-deaf, though certainly not always. Sometimes these white cats are born with a dark-to-black smudge mark on the forehead. It looks like a thumbprint, and often it disappears as the cat matures. Those cats born with the thumbprint, although they end up all-white and blue-eyed, are not deaf. You make what you want of that. (Whose thumbprint, for example, is it?) Although some people associate deafness with albinism, these white cats are not really albinos, since they do not have pink eyes.

The orange-eyed variety is easier to breed. It is not bedeviled with that hereditary hearing defect, and its eye color is easier to maintain generation after generation.

White short-haired cats breed true, but that is not their only source. They can show up among a litter of black kittens; and they can come from Tortoiseshells, or, for that matter, from any line where British Shorthair blood is likely to have been introduced.

White cats, long- or short-haired, have always held special fascination for people. They have been symbolic of purity, bringers of good luck, all kinds of things. Underneath that snowy coat (since a dirty white cat would be unthinkable, a little talcum powder can be used to help one keep clean) and behind those blue or orange eyes lives one of the world's most remarkable animals, the domestic cat of ancient and still-unknown origin.

Long-haired Cats: Long ago, Angora cats and Persian cats got all mixed up together in a beautiful big ball of fluff, and people have been arguing their generally no-longer-distinguishable virtues ever since. No matter, there is something especially aristocratic about a long-haired cat.

The early breeds of domestic cats in England had

short hair, as do so many today. In the late 1500s, something new was added. From Turkey and Persia, probably via France, a new kind of cat appeared and took at least the upper classes by storm (most sixteenth-century English working folk couldn't afford examples of the regal Persian and Angora cats). The Angora apparently came from Turkey and was then distinctly different from the Persian. The hair texture was quite different, also the shape of the head and face, but the two breeds were indiscriminately crossbred all through the 1600s and into the eighteenth century as well. It wasn't until the time of the American Civil War that breeders began to develop standards and studbooks. So the lines of today's Persian and Angora cats (both names are still in use) are inextricably crossed.

The ideal Longhair is expected to have a luxurious coat with a solid color of character and distinction. Nothing wishy-washy or indefinite will do. The round head should have a broad space between small, generously tufted ears. The cheeks should be full and round and self-satisfied looking, the nose short (kind of pushed in, really) and broad. The eyes must be very large and perfectly round. The coat is never woolly in a good specimen, but soft, silky, and extremely dense. The tail is relatively short and fully furred and never has a kink or break. The legs are short and solid, and the animal in the overall view should have a nice, square look.

While "solid color" is a breed standard, this doesn't mean the cat must be without markings, just that the colors should be assertive where they appear and add to the richness of the animal's overall appearance. All kinds of markings are allowed, even Siamese points and tortoiseshell, as well as the smoky solids, the rare reds, the creams, blues, and whites.

As recently as 1950, pure Angoras and Persians were

being listed and shown separately in the United States, with some people believing that the Angora was what later became known as the Coon cat and Maine cat. Some fanciers still insist the strains exist as pure lines today, while others insist they are mixed and were never separated, even in Persia. We are even told that the Persian cat was so rare in Persia there were none to be spared for export, and that what we call the Persian cat actually came from Afghanistan. It is one of those arguments that can go on forever. As for me, all I know is that what I see is beautiful, and beauty has always meant more to me than nomenclature.

Siamese Cat: If you like romantic stories, there is a creature you can buy for under fifty dollars that once upon a time might have cost you your head to own . . . perhaps, and then again, perhaps not.

The first Siamese cats were seen in England in the 1870s. It wasn't until 1903 that they turned up on our shores. They say the original cats were gifts from the king of Siam, where it was a crime punishable by death for a common man to own one. That could well be fantasy, for we are not even certain the Siamese cat originated in Siam; it could have come from India.

There is no more companionable creature than the Siamese cat. They are graceful and clean and one of the most satisfying of all pets. They are as demanding of your time as is a dog, and as affectionate and responsive to your care. Their blue-to-violet eyes and that soft coffee-and-cream coat with the elegant points make this animal a thing of beauty. Those points, by the way, can be chocolate, coffee, blue, red, frosty, lavender, or other exotic tones. Personally, I favor the common Seal Point. We have three Seal Points, and they are as different from each other as any three *people* I know.

Legends about the Siamese cat and its origins hold that it was a watch cat, and although that, too, is probably more legend than fact, there is no doubt that Siamese cats have very distinctive voices and are quick to let you know when a situation doesn't come up to their strict standards of how the world should be organized. One of our Siamese takes the ringing of the telephone as a personal affront and stalks around the room grumbling whenever it happens. She is even worse about a chiming clock.

I do believe that Siamese cats are best owned in pairs. They don't do well alone, especially if they are to be left during the day. And if you go out to buy a very young Siamese kitten, don't be surprised if you are offered an animal without those lovely dark Siamese points; they come later. Siamese kittens are born "blank" and get filled in as they grow.

You will find your Siamese cat, and this is true of *all* cats, more pleasant to live with if it is neutered; alter the male, spay the female. Unspayed Siamese females can drive you mad when they are in heat, for they are very highly motivated animals! Unaltered males can be a great deal of trouble. So unless you plan to open a Siamese cattery, get your cats neutered. You'll improve the quality of your pet's life *and* your own.

Manx Cat: If they gave out ribbons for the inspiration of nonsense stories, the Manx or Tailless cat would win them hands—paws—down. According to one story, Noah was in a hurry to slam the door on the ark because the rain had already begun to fall, and who should be the last animal on board but a cat who promptly got his tail cut off in the process—hence, the Manx cat. If that one is a bit much for you, how about the tailless cats that swam ashore on Britain's Isle of

Man when two ships of the Spanish Armada went down off Spanish Head? We could live with that one, except that the Spanish didn't have a strain of tailless cats, as far as we know, and we probably would know if they did. Perhaps the nicest tale concerns the warriors of the Isle of Man. They were jealous of the finery worn by their Irish or Danish foes and began cutting the tails off cats to adorn their helmets. Finally, one female cat, about to bear kittens, retreated to the top of Snaefell, the highest hill on the island. There she had her litter and bit their tails off so the warriors wouldn't molest them. She taught her daughters to do the same, and from that day on, Manx cats have been without tails. Only two things wrong there: acquired characteristics do not become hereditary, and Manx cats—that is, cats born to Manx—are not necessarily without tails. Two tailless Manx cats, bred together, may produce a mixed litter—some without tails, some with stunted tails, and some with perfectly normal ones. Indeed, too much in-breeding of tailless specimens can produce a fatal characteristic that kills the kittens almost as fast as they are born. In the words of the breeder, "tailless Manx cats do not breed true." But one has a show-quality Manx when the characteristic does appear. There should be no tail, none at all, in fact there should be a dent where the tail would normally be.

The hind legs of a Manx are a little longer than those of the average Tabby, and the rump is high and rounded. The coat is double—a thick, deep undercoat and a soft and silky outercoat. The body is compact, and the eyes should be full and very expressive. There is another bit of nonsense inspired by the Manx; it has been said, half seriously, that normal cats, cats with tails, waste a great deal of energy on their tails. In the case of the Manx, without a tail to sidetrack this mental energy, it has all gone to the cat's personality and intelligence. Nonsense, of course, but it makes owners of the Manx happy.

Those long hind legs, so characteristic of the breed, give the Manx a strange, hopping walk that has been described inaccurately as rabbitlike, although it is true that the Manx would rather hop over grass and weeds than plough through when hunting mice, a pastime it loves. The breed isn't all that friendly toward strangers, although it is affectionate and responsive with family members and other cats.

Manx cats are intelligent, alert, and active, and that orange-shaped rump, sans tail, is a conversation point. They are, by the way, becoming rare on the Isle of Man. Too many of the better specimens were shipped abroad in years past.

Abyssinian Cat: In 1876 and 1877 there was a senseless and brutal war between the British and Ethiopia. Home from that war came a British soldier bringing with him a strange cat. It was our first recorded Abyssinian cat. It had a brick-red nose, and each individual hair had three separate bands of color, producing an effect called ticking. With Abyssinians, there can be a fawn band at the base, then ruddy brick, and then either a black or very dark brown tip. The effect is rippling, an endless flow of color as the animal moves.

Where does the Abyssinian really come from? That's not easy to answer. Sacred cats of Egypt resembled the Abyssinian. Or it may have descended from the wild Caffre cat, a small native hunting cat of the Middle East and perhaps North Africa. In either case, the animal is probably three thousand years old.

The Abyssinian cat of today has many special characteristics besides a ticked coat. It loves to play in water and will even join you in your bath. It is extremely affectionate and highly active, in fact so active that you seldom see one relax. They are either on the go or sound asleep. They have sweet, bell-like voices, but are not talkative the way the Siamese are. They purr like express trains, though, and love people. They want to be with people all the time.

The first Abyssinian reached the United States, as far as we know, in 1930. Apparently, there were no offspring. In 1949 two more came, and the breed was established. Unfortunately, the Abyssinian is very expensive—you can easily spend $300 or more for an example, when you can find one for sale—so the breed is not everybody's cup of tea. Although it is a connoisseur's cat today, it is such an outstanding animal, one can safely predict that it will someday be popular and perhaps even common. After all, the Siamese was once nearly as rare. It is to be hoped that the demand for the Abyssinian and the desire of some breeders for quick money will not undermine the quality of this, one of the most beautiful of all domestic animals.

British Blue Cat: The British Blue is a big cat—big, sturdy, and muscular. They make first-rate pets, affectionate and frequently demonstrative.

The coat of the British Blue is not rough or harsh, but short, soft, and pleasant to the touch. This handsome cat should be unmarked, no shadings, no white hairs, no spots or streaks. There should be a light to medium blue color over the entire body. The eyes are huge and round. The expression is one of alert interest and basic good humor. Under certain conditions, you could swear the cat was smiling, or perhaps even laughing at you. The British Blue makes an exceptionally good parent. The breed is so in demand in the British

Isles that you usually have to get on a waiting list for a kitten.

The blue color has been carried over into other breeds. There are Blue Maltese, Blue Burmese, and Blue Chinchilla. There are Blue Creams in both the long- and short-haired cats and, of course, the Blue Point Siamese, which has been refined even further to a Lilac Point. There is also a Blue Tabby. In these cats, by the way, the word *blue* is not just a vague description; the color blue is distinctly that, clear and often bright, and to me at least, just a little surprising. Somehow, one expects colors like blue and purple among fish, frogs, and birds; but mammals, well, they are supposed to be brown and black and gray and shades of yellow and orange.

Russian Blue: The color is blue, right enough, but the breed probably originated in England, not Russia. It is the breed of cat they call the Russian Blue or the Archangel cat. Some people insist it is a Russian breed that spread to England via the Scandinavian countries, but there is no hard evidence of this, and probably we will never be able to sort the matter out.

The Russian Blue has large, pointed ears that are very wide at the base, very thin, and almost naked. Its color is bright blue and, in the adult cat, there should be no markings or shadings. No white is allowed by breed standards, though the lighter blues are preferred. The fur is short and thick and fine, and most pleasant to the touch. It has a sheen, is double, and should not lie flat. The texture and appearance of this coat is what distinguishes the breed.

The body of a Russian Blue is long and lithe and very graceful. The legs are long, and the feet are neat and small and well rounded. The face is broad, and the nose is of good length. The eyes should be as green as possible and look spectacular against the blue coat. If you get a Russian Blue kitten, you will have to wait a bit for the effect, since the cats are born with yellow eyes; in fact, it isn't until a Russian Blue is about two years old that you can expect its coat and eye color to be fully developed.

Russian Blues are imps, yet they can be quiet and pleasant to have around. They are expressive, happy, and affectionate cats, just about perfect pets. Unfortunately, they are also expensive and hard to find. True bloodlines have been difficult to hold intact, and good breeding stock is hard to locate. Still, if you want one of these lovely creatures badly enough, you will become familiar with the fancy and will track the breeders down, and then you will pay the price. Maybe there is a process of natural selection at work here: if you won't pursue the matter to the end, perhaps you don't deserve to own a Russian Blue. Be careful of pet-shop claims and casual breeders. Remember, your Russian Blue kitten won't develop until it is two years old, and whether or not you are going to end up with a rich blue cat with vivid green eyes depends on the honesty of the selling party. Buy carefully, buy from the specialty breeder. By the time your cat is two, you will love it no matter what it is. Unscrupulous sellers depend on that fact.

Korat Cat: The year was 1896, the place London, the event a cat show (something the British take very seriously). An exhibitor showed a blue cat with a heart-shaped face. Since the cat was reputed to have come from Thailand, and its breed was unknown, the judge passed on it as a strangely colored Siamese cat. The owner had a fit, but that was how matters were left. Actually, as we know now, the cat was a Korat. It wasn't until 1959 that a breeding pair of Korat cats was imported into the United States and not until 1966 that the breed was recognized.

The Korat is a beautiful cat. It has a lovely blue color with a silvery sheen that is quite distinctive. The face is heart shaped instead of the classical Siamese wedge, and the eyes are a brilliant green-gold. The ears are large and rounded. The body is strong and muscular, although only of medium size. The tail is of moderate length and may be straight or kinked in any number of ways. What the relationship of this cat is to the Siamese is not known. Some people claim the Korat is the ancestor of the Siamese, and it is true that when the two breeds are crossed, the Korat seems to predominate. Both breeds are said to come from Thailand, although that is highly questionable in the case of the Siamese, and the Korat, too, is very rare in that country.

It is even more rare here and in England. The demand is tremendous, and you can't just walk in and buy one. With luck, you can get on a waiting list, a long one, and then you had better have cash ready. But one can look ahead: in twenty years the Korat will be all the rage; the splendid blue cat with its silvery overtones will be readily available, as common as the Siamese is today. (Popularity has not made the Siamese any less handsome, personable, or desirable.) In the meantime, however, the Korat is a rare, expensive, and very exclusive animal, available only to the rich and the lucky. If you can't live without one, then buy a pet magazine, keep tabs on who is breeding and showing the Korat, and get your name on that list. Any good breeder will probably want to interview you first to see if you measure up to the cat. That's the way it should be with all animals.

Burmese Cat: England has given us all of the purebred cat lines we have today, with one notable exception. In 1930 the Western world learned of an incredibly lovely new breed of oriental cat, and the news spread from California, not London. The newcomer was the Burmese cat, and the importer was a Dr. G. C. Thompson. The cat was a female named Wong Mau.

People sometimes refer to the Burmese as a solid, dark Siamese. That is wrong. They are a breed apart. We first learned of them in India, and while their actual place of origin is unknown, it was probably not Burma.

The Burmese standard calls for lovely oval eyes, ideally a lustrous golden yellow in color. Breeders today are having trouble keeping out a greenish tint. The kittens are a light coffee color when they are young, but they mature into rich, sable brown, a lustrous color only slightly lighter on the belly. There is also a blue-gray variety of the breed called, not at all surprisingly, the blue Burmese. White markings are forbidden by breed standards.

The Burmese is a medium-sized cat, but is very strong, very muscular, and should never give the impression of being either fat or thin, just solid and powerful. The face is sweet, open, friendly, and inquisitive. Burmese are more solid in design than the somewhat leggier but equally lovely Siamese.

These fine breeds are the products of an enormous amount of love and attention. Maintaining breed standards is not a small job, for cats breed so readily that anyone who owns two cats can fancy himself a breeder. Get your Burmese from a top professional, a person with fierce pride. One way of distinguishing good breeders is the reluctance they exhibit when parting with one of their kittens. A real breeder hates to let one go. Beware the merchant who is anxious to move supposedly purebred stock.

The Burmese cat is not an inexpensive animal—prices in the hundreds are to be expected for a good specimen (and don't blanch when you find out how many hundreds). Not everyone can own a Burmese cat, and not everyone should. They are still rare, still the breed for the serious cat lover—a living collector's piece for the connoisseur. When you finally get to know someone else's Burmese, you will understand why . . . and probably go out and get one for yourself.

Alley Cat: He is properly called the Domestic Shorthair, but he is nothing more than a mixed-breed, or what we sometimes call an alley cat. In a way distinctly his own he is king of them all. In my home, we have a Tabby, he belongs to my daughter Pamela, and his somewhat ponderous name is Marshmallow Merrymole Meep—Meep for short. He is a perfectly splendidlooking tom, and he lords it over our nine other cats—Angora, Siamese, and alley cats alike. He is as elegant as the purest bred of them, and they respect him for what he is, Lord and Master. They bathe him and defer to him when it comes to sunny windowsills. He is a gentle lord, fair but firm, the kind of benevolent king that I would have rule over me, if I had to have a king. That's our Meep, with the *M* in the middle of his forehead. . . .

Meep is a milk drinker, but he would never deign to dip his head in the bowl. Meep daintily dips the end of his right paw into the milk and laps it off. It is the only way he will drink it. How's that for class?

What I am trying to show, of course, is that the common Domestic Shorthair is one of the greatest pet animals of them all, one that costs pennies when he costs anything. Every year millions of alley cats are born for which there never will be any homes. By the tens of thousands they are stuffed into gas chambers or drowned in sacks loaded down with rocks, and by the same numbers they starve or are crushed beneath speeding wheels. If you can take an alley cat, or two or three, into your life, you will literally be saving lives. And then, most important, get those cats altered. Not to alter a cat is to condemn many innocent animals to terrible deaths. True, an alley cat has a better chance of survival in the wild than most other domestic animals, but those chances are still thin enough to make abandonment to fate a clear act of cruelty. Remember, too, that cats are animal eaters. They can't help that, and a cat prowling for a living is a cat that will kill birds and small mammals.

If your array of pets doesn't include a Domestic Shorthair, it's just not complete. They can be great with kids, great with other animals, and a pleasure to have around. If you've never had one, you are in for a big surprise. They are nowhere near as independent as you probably think. Treat them right, and they'll respond with an affection you never knew existed.

Feline Panleucopenia: Feline panleucopenia is a highly contagious viral disease of cats, raccoons, and other mammals. It is often called feline distemper, although the virus involved is not related to the true canine distemper virus. "Panleuc" is also called "feline enteritis" and "cat plague." The disease has a short incubation period, usually about one week. It is very infectious, especially to young, unprotected cats. For just this reason, *never* put an unvaccinated cat on the floor or bench in a veterinarian's waiting room.

The disease can be so violent that by the time you realize something is wrong it is too late. Usually, though, there is a series of symptoms in progression. High fever comes first—often up to 105 degrees—with listlessness, lack of interest in food, vomiting, inability to drink or keep water down, diarrhea, and dehydration. The panleucopenia virus is tough and persistent, and after the disease has occurred in a home, six months should elapse before a new cat is introduced. At no time should unvaccinated cats be exposed to other cats.

There is a reliable vaccine available, and all cats must receive it as soon as possible. The first shot is usually given at eight weeks. Around ten weeks the second shot can be given, and the third will come between twelve and sixteen weeks of age. If you do not have the kitten at eight weeks, the veterinarian may want to vary that schedule, but generally, two or three shots are required. Most important is the last shot—it has to come after the kitten reaches a certain plateau. Each veterinarian has his own system, and the important thing is that he or she have the option to decide what is best for your pet. That means placing the animal in the veterinarian's care as early as possible.

Panleucopenia has a very high mortality rate, but it is not inevitably fatal. Its treatment does require antibiotics and all manner of supportive medicine. The diarrhea has to be stopped, dehydration dealt with, and the fever reduced. The animal will need vitamins, food supplements, and other therapy. You can do it at home—indeed, some veterinarians want you to because you will be your own animal's best nurse—but it must be done under the veterinarian's guidance and supervision.

Cat Nutrition: Although we still know far too little about companion-animal nutrition, a lot of research is going on in the field. Here are some basic facts about the cat: a cat tends to develop preferences, so it is wise to start your cat off on a good balanced diet and keep it there. The ideal cat diet will contain at least thirty percent protein; fats, minerals, vitamins, and carbohydrates will fill out the ration. Cooked carbohydrates can be utilized by a cat as an energy source. Personally, I think it is dangerous to include much canned fish in cats' diets, even though they may like it. An awful lot of people feel it shortens their lives. They don't seem able to assimilate it. Most canned-fish diets for cats contain scrap tuna, and that is just not a good food for the house cat. We have to learn more about this.

Cats are by nature irregular or intermittent feeders, and it is perfectly all right for an adult cat to skip a day or two. Still, such a cat should be watched, for the surest sign that he may be coming down with something is if he goes off his feed for long. It is almost impossible to get a cat to eat when it doesn't feel well. Also, a cat off food may be risking dehydration, which can lead to serious problems.

For the first six months of a kitten's life, it is just about impossible to overfeed it. Since a dietary or calorie deficiency will inhibit growth, you should watch that in the little ones—feed them up. Solid food need not be delayed beyond four weeks at the most, and many people like to start them a little earlier. If weight gain isn't up to snuff, or if there are true dietary deficiencies, you are asking for such troubles as acute respiratory and gastric disorders.

A newborn kitten weighs about a quarter of a pound, but by one week should be close to a pound. By five to ten weeks of age that weight doubles, and by the time a kitten is thirty weeks old, six and a half to seven pounds is normal. That takes a lot of food, much more than the queen can supply in her milk beyond a month.

There are lots of good cat foods on the market, both moist (where you pay for water and the can) and dry. Find the one, two, or three your cat likes, and feed it right. Many cat owners set food out and let their cats eat ad lib, which they will do unless there are other animals to give them a feeling of competition. Water should be available at all times. If dry foods are used, only those with low ash content should be considered. Check the labels for content. Avoid foods that do not specify ash content, for it is believed that too much ash can contribute to urinary disorders.

A properly fed cat can easily pass twenty years, all other things being equal, and some have made thirty.

The Litter Box: A very important appurtenance in the cat-owning household is the litter box. Life without one is unimaginable (unless you don't own a cat). The box should be positioned so that it is available to your pet twenty-four hours a day. You cannot restrict your cat to some schedule you devise. If you must lock your cat in one room when you go out, or because you have guests who are allergic, put the cat box where the cat is. Continued unavailability of a litter box may start your cat on a very bad downhill course. Faced with constant or frequent necessity, it may simply forget its natural instincts and start using pillows, planters, and other undesirable surrogate toilets. That can be hard to reverse once started.

What you put in the box is not as important as how often you clean it. Shredded newspaper is fine, cheap, and always available. Slick magazine paper is less desirable since it is not absorbent enough and tends to form a soggy mass; your cat can't kick it around and tidy up. The various clay products collectively called "litter" are probably best. As for brand, pick one that isn't too dusty. When you pour it, there should be no cloud of fine particles hovering over it. Many cats have a respiratory allergy to that kind of dust. Large bags are a lot cheaper by unit weight.

Clean the cat box often. Litter can generally be flushed right down the toilet and will not clog pipes. It is a good idea to wash the box out even if it does not seem soiled after the litter has been poured away. It will be less objectionable to you and, perhaps more importantly, to your cat. A litter box that is always nasty can turn a cat off, and a turned-off cat can, again, develop alternative procedures you will not appreciate.

The cat box should be placed, if possible, in a quiet and even concealed place. In our house, we were able to cut through a wall and provide a cat-sized passage into the garage where the cat box is contained in a special cabinet we built there. That way, we can carry the litter box outside without trekking it through the house, and the cats have the privacy they prefer (it does not help a cat's dignity to be charged by a dog when in that particular position). A little imagination can make a cat box less conspicuous, and regular cleaning can make it seem as if it wasn't there at all. Be sure to wash your hands after servicing your cat's toilet. Enough said.

Cats Scratching Furniture: Some cats take to clawing furniture and drapes, and the resulting damage can be expensive. First, you have to understand why cats do it. It is perfectly normal behavior. Cats do it to remove a rough, worn claw and to expose the fresh new claw that has grown up underneath; they also do it for fun and exercise, and, perhaps, out of occasional boredom.

If you build or buy a scratching post for a young kitten and keep it near its normal sleeping place, you can usually get the kitten onto the post very early. Scratching is often associated with stretching when a cat wakes up, so putting a post near its bed is a good rule. If you catch your cat scratching furniture, you can move it over to the post and wean it away from the bad habit. Some cats seem to prefer a rough fabric, and some like a log with bark. The former is a little cleaner in the house, but you may have to experiment and find which is most attractive to your cat.

Some people have very successfully combined a scratching post with a play unit by running a rug-covered pole from floor to ceiling and tiering it with platforms and passage holes. If the litter box is nearby, a cat would probably use such a unit for much of its active time during the day.

Cats are going to scratch *some*thing, but *not* out of destructive malice. Any destruction that does occur will be the result of perfectly normal feline behavior, motivated by a simple physical need. There are relatively rare cases where nothing you can do will work. The cat simply will not leave your furniture alone (and one cat can do three or four hundred dollars' worth of damage in one night). Declawing can be resorted to, but (as suggested later) that is a last resort only. It is painful (after the operation, not during it) and is not normal pet-care procedure. It is something you should discuss with your veterinarian if no other solution works.

When Your Cat Sheds: Cats do shed, and it can be a nuisance for the meticulous housekeeper and an absolute agony for an allergic person. No one knows all of the factors in shedding, except that it is normal. It does vary with the season—the extra-long hairs fall out as the temperature warms up. When cats are kept inside all year long, that pattern is disrupted, and in such cases, a cat can shed twelve months of the year. Artificial heat can be very drying, and shedding can increase as a result. Light intensity and hormone balance may also influence the amount of shedding. And some cats lose great quantities of hair as a reaction to stress, such as hospitalization or boarding.

If it seems to you that your cat is shedding more than normal, you can take two steps on your own. The cat can be brushed at least once a day with a regular cat brush that you can buy in a pet shop. Go with the growth—most cats hate being brushed against the grain. A rough cloth mitten is easy to make and can be used to stroke the cat vigorously. It provides a nice cat-owner interaction, as well as a measure of control on excess hair. If the skin and coat seem dry, oil can be added to the diet—call your veterinarian, and ask him to suggest supplements. If the shedding is really abnormal, and if plenty of brushing and diet supplements haven't done any good, your veterinarian should see your pet. He may want to take additional steps on a professional level.

Cat hair is not a joke—it can be irritating on clothing and furniture, and it does make some people very uncomfortable and others extremely ill. Some shedding will always occur, and any seriously allergic guests are going to get into trouble the minute they walk into the house. It is a good idea to keep a fresh bottle of strong antihistamines on hand in case someone does show up for dinner who is allergic. They may not know you have a cat and come without their own medication. A couple of antihistamines can save an evening.

Cats and Birds: We see photographs from time to time, in a newspaper centerfold or magazine, of a cat with a canary sitting on its head. Certainly there are exceptions to every rule, and cat versus bird is just one more rule. But don't count on this exception. Think rather in terms of your cat being the avowed enemy of all feathered creatures. It is unfair to birds to approach the situation otherwise, and it can be unfair to your cat. More than one person has had his cat killed or simply disappear because he would not face the problem of its going after his neighbor's bird feeder.

Some cats go stark crazy when they see a bird or even hear one. Perhaps you have seen a Siamese sitting on the windowsill with its bottom jaw quivering as it uttered the strangest sounds of frustration and desire. The cat can't help that. In the wild, the bird would be natural prey, and cats can't turn their instincts off as easily as dogs can, at least so it seems. The way birds move—in quick, sudden movements—also turns cats on; it makes the feathered creature an even more tempting target, for practice if not for food. Don't get angry with your cat. Try to control it. If you found it hard to quit smoking and your own kid or nephew can't stop biting his fingernails, why should you expect a cat to give up birds?

Keep birds and cats apart: that is the basic rule. If your cat goes out, bell it—on a breakaway, safety cat collar. Don't let it wander onto a neighbor's property and use it as a hunting ground. That is an insult to your neighbor and a hazard to your cat.

If you also have a pet bird, don't put its cage where it can be sent rocketing to the floor with great regularity under the assault of your feline in a feather frenzy. And don't put it where it has to watch your cat stalk its cage for hours on end. That is just plain cruel.

I don't know anyone who has found a way of making

birds uninteresting to cats. Some cats are so socially evolved they aren't interested, but these are exceptions. There is no such thing as a convert. A hunter is a hunter all of its days.

Cat Fights: Many cats tend to fight. Unaltered males do so with great regularity, and some toms become very aggressive bullies, wandering the neighborhood looking for trouble. Many cats simply do not like other cats and will attack without warning when a stranger intrudes on their territory.

Since cat-fight injuries can be dangerous and frequently disfiguring, the best cure for the cat fight is prevention. The first logical step is neutering. When you alter a male, you are solving many cat-owning problems. And by spaying your female, you will obviate the inviting aroma that can bring strange cats into your yard. The second obvious rule is, don't let your cats wander. Those that do wander tend to have very short lives, so here again more than one purpose is served. If you know you own a bully, be doubly careful to keep him at home, not only for the good of your neighbors' animals, but because a bully always gets his own in the end.

Cats are not as responsive to verbal commands as are dogs, so you can't depend on your voice to break up a fight. Two devices usually work. An extremely loud noise can do it. Pick up an empty garbage pail, and throw it down near the fighting cats, or slam together a couple of garbage-pail lids, like a pair of cymbals. The second device is water. It is amazing what a bucket of cold water will do to the disposition of even the fightin'est cat. The one thing you most certainly should *not* do is stick your hands into the middle of the fray. When cats fight they go just a bit berserk, and you can almost depend on getting slashed if you physically intrude upon a cat fight.

See to a cat's fight injuries promptly; often that means a visit to the vet. Cat claws are generally loaded with bacteria, and injured cats can become abscessed or worse. Your veterinarian may want to use antibiotics or do some fancy stitching. And if you have two cats in one household that really fight—I don't mean the kind of normal carrying-on that occurs when a new cat is introduced—but if they really and continually have at each other, you probably should think of finding a new home for one of them.

Cats are highly motivated, highly emotional animals —emotional in their own sense, not ours—and some can be dreadful fighters. Such situations take watching and some intelligent application on the part of the owners.

First Aid for Cats: There are times when cats require emergency first aid, but remember, first aid is just that —aid that you give first, before getting to a veterinarian, because the cat can't wait for professional help.

Bleeding, as always, is the first consideration following an accident. If it does not stop on its own, then a pressure bandage might be needed. As a last resort, a tourniquet can be put on a limb or a tail. It must be loosened every fifteen minutes, however.

After bleeding, shock is the main concern. Shock can kill an animal as small as a cat very quickly. An animal showing signs of shock should be kept warm and quiet and be put into the hands of a veterinarian as soon as possible. If the cat seems to be in shock, a good way to test is to press on the cat's gum with one finger. The gum will turn white under your finger, and in a normal cat, if you lift your finger away, the white area will turn pink again in a second or two; if it takes longer than that, there is poor blood return, and shock is probably present.

Artificial respiration can be given to an unconscious cat. Set the cat upright on its stomach, and take a deep breath. Hold the cat's mouth closed, cover its muzzle with your mouth, and exhale. Pull back and let the cat exhale. Its chest should have inflated when you blew. Repeat this about six times a minute until the cat can breathe on its own.

In case of suspected poisoning, it is again important that a veterinarian see the animal as soon as possible. It is also very important that you bring with you the container of whatever the cat has ingested so the doctor can determine exactly what it is and exactly what he should do to counteract its effects.

Simple cuts and tears can be treated just as in a human being. The area should be cleaned, shaved if necessary, covered with an antiseptic, and then bandaged. If the bandage is too uncomfortable, the animal will tear it away, so try to use moderation and good sense. Normal cuts will dry up and stop bleeding in five to ten minutes. Anything beyond that could spell trouble.

Don't call your veterinarian out of bed in the middle of the night for something that can wait until the next day, but emergencies are emergencies and must be seen to by professionals. Watch for bleeding, shock, and poisons—they are the quick killers. [See also "First Aid for Dogs," pp. 62–64.]

Altering and Declawing: It is common practice today to physically alter living animals, surgically alter them, so that they can fit into our lives without being disruptive forces. This seems to upset a lot of people. I must confess that I am rarely among them. Some cats like to sharpen their claws on heavy textured surfaces, like the arms and fronts of couches and chairs, or on rugs. The damage a cat can do can run into thousands of dollars in one evening. And then, as an even worse consequence, the cat may be kicked out, put down, or abandoned by owners who are too pure in their belief in "natural" animals to revert to surgery. Sorry, but I think such an attitude is nonsense. While an unaltered cat living as nature created him may seem desirable, no one should have to have his house in tatters, and no cat should be put down or thrown out because he likes to sharpen his claws the way nature intended him to. Any veterinarian can remove the cat's front claws—just the front ones have to go—while the animal is under a general anesthetic. If a couple of days, the cat is home, and in a week, the stitches are out. It can be done, in fact usually is done, at the same time the cat is neutered or spayed. Impure, yes, eminently sensible, yes, when a cat will not use a scratching post. And there are cats like that. There is the counterconsideration that if your cat is to be allowed to roam (not a good practice if you want your cat to grow old), he can be at a disadvantage if attacked. He will be short on fighting-back equipment and will be slow going up a tree, although most declawed cats still manage to climb pretty well. This is not a consideration in house cats. Declawing should certainly be the last resort, but some cats will simply not use a scratching post, and in those cases, there may be no other way. Only then should it be done.

Some people resort to having canine teeth removed so that they won't get bitten badly. That's one I can't buy. Protecting furniture is one thing, protecting yourself against your own pet is silly. In that case, you have the wrong pet to begin with.

As for desexing, by whatever name you want to use, altering, neutering, spaying, whatever, there is no argument. People should be required to destroy the reproducing potential of any animal for which they have not obtained a breeding license. Anyone who argues about the "impurity" of sexually altering animals has never been in the back room of a pound. Well, I have. I used to work there, and I say, spay away and alter, too.

There is a lady by the name of Phyllis Wright who works for The Humane Society of the United States. When people allow surplus puppies and kittens to be born, she challenges them on why they haven't had their pets spayed. The usual answer is that they want their children to see the miracle of birth. Her answer is, "Take your children along when you have to take your next litter to your veterinarian to dispose of them for you. He can take them into the back room and introduce them to the miracle of death." It makes them stop and think.

Just to reiterate, declawing is a last resort. It should only be done when there is no other way short of getting rid of a pet. Spaying and altering are first steps and something all cat owners, except professional breeders, should have done for all of their pets.

Essay on the Cat: A gentleman once asked me why I owned a cat. How does one answer such a question? I will try.

I own a cat because I love a mystery. I own a cat because I think that life is good.

Perhaps those of us who own cats find in them some ancient truths, perhaps we admire the dignity of the beast. Most people who speak of cats as independent never owned a cat, I'm quite sure. Cats, in their way, are as dependent as dogs. It is just that, as individualists, they have their own style of eloquence, their own way of letting you know. A cat is beautiful, of course, and it makes as much sense to own one beautiful thing as another. If a man cannot understand why you own a cat, I guess he would be befuddled by your Van Gogh or your Rembrandt. Of course, a Rembrandt or a Van Gogh can be reproduced by photography or lithography or some other technical means. But no cat has ever been reproduced, no two cats are altogether alike, any more than any two people are.

The man who asked me why I owned a cat wasn't challenging me, not really. If he had been, I would not have deigned to answer. But I don't mind trying to impart an impression, a feeling, a reason why I think a cat is good, in the hopes that somewhere, someone will read this and be nicer to a cat than they were before. Cats have been with man for thousands of years and have answered a need—more than one, really, for they are more than mousers, more than decorative bits of living procelain. They are friends to shut-ins, to older people, to children. Cats don't take up room, they aren't noisy, they are as clean as can be, and they respond to the softer side of human nature. That in us which is bad and harsh and mean gets no response from a cat, only that which is humane and good and calm. In that sense, perhaps, the cat is a governor on our speeding lifestyles. I have seen men harsh with the stress of their lives grow soft and quiet in the presence of a cat. Anything that can temper our rage must be good, physically and emotionally good, not just for us but for those around us.

5

OTHER PETS

The Horse as a Pet: Many people are interested in horses or at least in buying a horse for a child. It makes sense to think about the matter before mistakes get made. Horses are among the most beautiful of animals, and the most appealing. They can also be expensive, heartbreaking, and dangerous. It is a good idea to get one's head in order before taking out the checkbook. You can buy a saddle horse, depending on the season (cheaper in fall and winter than in spring and summer) for $75, and you can buy one for $25,000. The difference lies in your taste, needs, and ability to pay.

No horse should be purchased until it has been examined by your own veterinarian and given a clean bill of health. "Vetting"—and it is the standard term even among veterinarians themselves—means having an animal thoroughly examined prior to purchase, and if you anticipate buying a horse, it is an essential step. Horses, despite their size and power, are subject to many tricky ailments—some that you would never be able to recognize yourself. In many areas of the country, a horse should be given the Coggins test to be certain it is free of equine infectious anemia or swamp fever. It must be checked for soundness, its wind must be right, and above all, its feet must be inspected. The horse runs on one toe, and its foot is one of the most complicated anatomical structures in the animal kingdom. Look at that single toe—a horse weighing half a ton must slam it to earth hundreds and hundreds of times every time it is ridden. If your horse is a jumper, its entire weight must come down on two toes every time it gives you a fence or wall. It has been said that if the human foot with its present design were to take the punishment a horse's single toe does, it would have to be the size of a tennis court to survive.

It is sad to think of the fate of an unsound horse, but an animal that size is too large an investment for you to go into it blindly. You should never entertain the idea of buying a horse or pony until you have hired your own equine practitioner, your own veterinarian with a special interest in horses, and taken him to see the horse, no matter where it is. And there is this to consider, too—any seller who objects when you say you will be bringing your veterinarian to examine the horse is automatically suspect; no professional would have any respect for your judgment and your intelligence if you went about it any other way.

Next, be sure you know what it costs to stable a horse where you live, or what hay, feed, and grain cost if you are going to do the horse-keeping yourself. In some parts of the country, horse board runs as low as $35 a month, while in other places, it is $250 a month. Be certain you know how much it is around where you live and that you can get a stable for your horse once you buy it. Make sure your youngster, if that's whom the horse is for, has been properly trained, not only in horse riding, but also in horse-keeping, for that is an important part of it. A horse is an investment. No one should ever buy a horse as a pet. Keep saying that over and over again; be very firm with yourself. I know whereof I speak, for I said it over and over about my daughter's first horse, and that is why Alexander, now retired, is retired on me, and I get the bill for his board every month. Still, it was worth it, he taught my daughter all she knows. He was patient and careful when she, as a novice, was more vulnerable. His gentleness made her very survival possible during those learning years. Horses aren't pets . . . horses aren't pets . . . and good luck to you as a first-time horse owner.

Keep Your Own Horse: Many people today are quite willing to buy their youngster a horse, but are discouraged by the high cost of boarding in some parts of the country. You can buy a decent horse in one state for what it will cost you to board it for one month in another. Is it possible to keep a horse yourself? Yes, if you have the room and the time.

Two questions must be answered first: Where will the horse be kept at night and in bad weather? and Where in the daytime and in good weather? You have to have satisfactory answers to both questions. A garage, a shed, a barn, or other outbuilding can make a decent box stall if it is properly protected from the weather, and if it is reasonably solid and can be maintained. It should, obviously, have a firm floor. It is also necessary to have storage facilities for hay, straw, feed, and tack. Running water is also a necessity.

Even more expensive than converting a shed or garage into a stall is the problem suggested by that second question: Where is the horse kept when the weather is good? Outside is the answer, and fencing is the problem. A horse should have a decent area to move around in and graze. Fencing does not mean some strings of barbed wire tacked to trees. Fencing means posts set in the ground and wooden rails. It means a proper gate that can be secured and can be opened wide enough to allow a horse to pass through comfortably and safely. Barbed wire may be fine when you are fencing whole herds on thousands of acres, but a single horse in a small area is going to get hung up and badly hurt sooner or later if you use wire. Safety is a major concern. So is escape. The fence has to be both high enough and secure enough to hold the animal, even when a passing truck backfires or a fire truck or ambulance goes screaming by.

Anyone really interested in setting up some light

horse-keeping on his own property should hire an experienced horse person, or better yet, a veterinarian, to come over and look around and offer an hour or two's consultation. Go into it with some good solid advice from people who know the problems and have been through it themselves.

Horsemanship for Your Child: It may seem hard to believe, but there are more saddle horses in private ownership in America today than there were at the turn of the century. And interest in horsemanship and horse shows is on the increase. Horse shows, by the way, unlike the typical dog bench show (but not unlike dog field trials), center more around the things a horse can do, or a horse and rider can do together.

A great many fathers and mothers each year are faced with urgent appeals by their children that a horse is the thing they want most in this world, the only thing that will make them really happy, and the last big thing they will ever ask for. The pattern is typical and constitutes one of the best-developed games around. It usually starts when the child is between eight and ten and, if unsatisfied, is apt to continue into the late teens. The chances run about eighty percent that it will be a daughter making the request. Should you buy your child a horse? The decision is a very personal one and really depends on the ability to pay and the desire to become involved in a major new activity. It is not to be taken lightly.

These are a few guidelines that can be helpful if you decide to give in. Personally, I am against buying a child a horse during the first year of enthusiasm. That makes it too easy, does not make a horse something that is achieved. And it can be a foolish expenditure if the enthusiasm wanes, as it sometimes does, when a child finds out how much work is involved in taking a show ribbon of any color, much less a blue or tricolor championship. For the first year, let the child try a school that supplies the horse, and see if he or she does progress and does warrant that horse-size investment. Now, what to buy and how much to spend? First, there is no justification for buying a stallion. It isn't necessary and can be dangerous. That leaves mares and geldings, and either is satisfactory. Don't think ponies are cheaper than horses, for in animals suitable for showing, one can cost as much as the other. Horses generally, but *not* always, are a little milder mannered than good ponies with show potential. Personally, I don't think it wise to start youngsters out with their ultimate horse, the horse they dream of riding in Madison Square Garden. During their early riding years, a horse of real show quality is apt to be too much for them to handle. Get a first horse first, a mild-mannered, somewhat experienced schooling horse, and let your child grow into the hotter Arabs and Thoroughbreds later.

The cost of your child's horse or pony will vary. A couple of hundred dollars can get your child a lot of time and fun in the saddle. Start out on the low side, and worry about a solid-gold Thoroughbred later.

I know of no pastime, no hobby, no interest that requires a greater degree of concentration and dedication to self-improvement than horsemanship. But the rewards can be great, and what, after all, really is the price you should put on anything today that leads your child into channels of self-discipline and the determination to accomplish perfection?

Danger in Horsemanship: "My daughter is dying to have a horse," the letter began, "but I don't want her to die because I gave in." The gentleman was worried, and that is understandable. How dangerous is horsemanship?

I won't swear to it, but I think this is so: horse shows send kids into the game with less protective gear than is prescribed for any other major sport in America today except tennis and golf. Youngsters riding a thousand and twelve hundred pounds of horse into jumps three or more feet high wear nothing more protective than a hard hat, and it isn't at all certain how protective those are. An awful lot of parents deny their children this sport because of the risks. Now both of my kids have had horses and ridden in shows. Does that make me an indifferent parent? I don't think so, and I sweat out every round on that outside course every show of the year. The difference for both my wife and me, the way we try to give our youngsters maximum protection, is to get them professional training. I am against amateurism in this field. It is just too hazardous. Kids need expert training in riding and horse management if they are to play the game with a safety margin. Anyone who says horses aren't potentially dangerous, at least as they are ridden in shows, doesn't know his animals. Horses, forgive me for saying this, aren't bright. I don't know that I would call them stupid, the way some people do, but bright they are not. They frighten easily. Not long ago my own daughter was riding a superbly trained saddle horse, an animal on which she has won over eighty ribbons, and a cement mixer passed nearby. Her horse went nearly mad with fear, and, despite my daughter's skill and experience, she almost lost her head as the horse took the nearest escape route under a tree with low branches.

I have seen a score of youngsters get thrown or go over jumps their mounts have refused, and although there is no such thing as one-hundred-percent insur-

ance, the kids with expert training have a better chance
of coming out in one piece. They know how to land,
how to roll, how to disengage when a horse stumbles.
I have seen my own youngster go over a horse's head
when it suddenly shied at a hard canter and land on
her feet at a full run, without so much as dropping
the reins. Expert training means command of the situation, command that gets through to the horse in the
first two minutes the rider is aboard.

Expert training does not mean an hour or two with a
groom at a local hack stable. It means qualified judges
and teachers and lots of practice. There is no substitute,
nothing that will take the place of training and hard
work.

A child who is encouraged to show a horse without
the necessary schooling (of both horse and rider) is
being placed in jeopardy. You wouldn't let your youngsters go skin diving, or even boating, unless they could
swim well. Give them the same break if riding is the
game. Training by experts is the only way it should be
done.

Pony Breeds: It looks good on paper, but the difference
between a pony and a horse is not always that easy
to establish. According to the rules, a pony's height at
the withers doesn't exceed fifty-eight inches, or fourteen hands two in horsey parlance. But that does not
always hold. Some Arabs and Quarter horses, although
of pony size, are shown as horses, while polo ponies
and cow ponies may be horse size. It can be confusing.

The ponies that are ponies we call the pony breeds.
From Austria comes the handsome Haflinger, a mountain pony, surefooted and strong, an animal once used
to pack hay down from mountain meadows. Poland has

given us the Konik, good-tempered, willing, long-lived, and very fertile. Poland also gave the world the Huzul, sturdy, of great endurance, and very, very hardy. Germany had a pony known as the Dülmen, which runs today in semiwild herds in Westphalia. From Spain comes a pony known as the Sorraia or Garronos, a crude and scrubby-looking beast, very primitive in appearance.

Sweden has given us a pony known as the Gotland, which is handsome and exceptionally hardy and quick, though examples do tend to be pigheaded. Norway has the Fjord pony, a small animal with exceptional muscles and with a characteristically upstanding mane. Another Norwegian contribution is the Northlands pony, which is small-headed and very hardy. Iceland gives us the docile Iceland pony. The small, oriental-looking pony seen in Greece is the Peneia, and the somewhat sleeker-looking critter is the Pindos. The Greek pony that looks more like a donkey than a small horse is the Skyros.

There are many others, of course—the Viatka and the Karabakh from Russia; the Exmoor from England, the New Forest and Dartmoor, the Fell and the Dales, the Welsh Mountain, the Welsh, the Highland and the Shetland, and dozens of others—all British ponies. All have descended from the basic horse stock and developed into smaller animals to better take advantage of the world they were destined to inhabit.

Ponies generally are tougher than horses, much hardier, and less tractable. In fact, most ponies are harder to handle, allowing for size difference, of course. Still, around the world, ponies are owned and ridden and loved by kids. Unfortunately, ponies have been among the most ill treated of animals. Do you own a pony? How do you treat it? Give the little beast a break.

Shetland Pony: He is small, and he is tough, and he can be gentle as a lamb, if you like the idea of a lamb under saddle. He can also be as ornery and stubborn as a mule. We refer to neither the lamb nor the mule, but the cross between the two (figuratively speaking), the Shetland pony.

When the Romans pulled out of England in 410 A.D., they left behind a number of their horses running wild in a then-wild land. Newly free, they spread out and filtered into the hills to the north, into what is now Scotland. No one seems to have any idea how, but some of them reached the Shetland Islands two hundred miles off Scotland's north coast. One thing seems certain, they didn't swim. They must have been carried there by someone. Eventually they adapted themselves to their new home—they got even smaller, for life on those exposed islands can be pretty grim, forage can be short, and winter can be long. What emerged was the Shetland pony. The other, more refined horses that later began reaching the British Isles were not carried across to the Shetlands, so the ponies there didn't benefit from the new bloodlines, though they seem to have done all right on their own. Champion examples have sold for as much as $50,000.

Shetlands come in a variety of colors and characteristically have long, flowing manes and tails. They should be up to forty-six inches tall. Most Shetlands are reasonably gentle and reliable and are known for their intelligence. Surefooted by nature, they are hardy in almost any weather and as strong as little donkeys. They don't require a lot of fancy feed to hold their condition, and all of this, plus their size, makes them close to ideal for small children. One other thing, they are exceptionally long-lived. At thirty many are still being ridden, and some have lasted until forty, about twice the useful life you would expect from most horses. I have known Shetlands to be mean, but they were the exception. For small children, the Shetland can be the answer. Of course children do grow up, and it doesn't take many years for kids to outgrow a forty-six-inch mount; and, as Confucius say, "Tall kid on a short horse take precious few ribbons." So a Shetland can have that disadvantage, unless you have a string of kids coming along to inherit the noble mount.

Welsh Mountain Pony: When the Roman legions withdrew from Wales, they left behind bands of hardy horses, as they did in what is now England. A breed that had been developed in North Africa, the bands became feral, semiwild. In time, new blood was infused into their line by Andalusians from Spain and Barbs, Arabs, and Turks from the east. All of these animals were of fair size, but as with the Shetland, the rugged conditions under which they had to exist in the Welsh hills resulted in a reduction in size. What evolved was a miniature horse of almost unbelievable endurance and resourcefulness. Today we know that miniature horse, an animal of forty-six to forty-eight inches and under six hundred pounds, as the Welsh Mountain pony.

The studbook for the Welsh Mountain came into being in 1903, and the line has been improved by selective breeding on farms and by turning desirable stallions loose to assemble their own harems of feral mares. The Welsh Mountain pony is in every sense a child's horse, with few of the personality faults of other ponies. It has the stability and personality of the best breeds of saddle horse, while retaining a size that is handy for the junior hunter. Welsh ponies jump well, and they perform well under saddle or in harness in any division practical to their size. Some of the best

riders this country has ever seen started out on a good
Welsh pony.

Characteristically, they have well-spaced, alert, and
intelligent eyes, a slightly concave face, and are usually
bay, black, brown, cream, or dun; most often they are
gray. The Welsh Mountain pony should not be piebald
or skewbald. They are known for their docility. They
like children and respond well to intelligent handling.
Some can be so finely trained that they will not respond
well to a novice, but generally they are almost never
touchy. They subsist well under rough conditions and
get along on relatively little fodder. They are, in a word,
tough.

Thoroughbred Horse: A so-called thoroughbred dog is
a purebred animal of any recognized breed in its species. A Thoroughbred horse is also purebred, but of a
specific type or breed. There is only one Thoroughbred
horse, and he is known as "the Thoroughbred."

The history of the Thoroughbred, as a recognized
breed, goes back to England in the late 1600s. There a
horse known as the Byerly Turk (a Turk is a mixture
of Arab, Persian, and other Asiatic breeds) and an
Arabian known as the Darley Arabian were established
into a line and crossed into other lines based on an
Arabian foaled about 1724 and known as the Godol-
phin Arabian. Native English breeds like the Galloway,
Highland Dun, and Scotch pony were crossed in
through the mares and, slowly, the magnificent Thoroughbred as we know him now emerged. He was a
carefully, even meticulously constructed animal whose
characteristics can be traced all the way back to those
early days of experimentation. It is safe to say that the
Thoroughbred line has produced the most valuable individual animals in the world, for it is the Thorough-

bred one sees on the tracks of England and the United States. The breed is also the favorite in horse shows; most people who show horses, unless they are showing in specialty classes or other-breed shows, feel that without a Thoroughbred, you don't stand much of a chance with the judges.

There are many variations on the central theme— American Thoroughbreds, Irish Thoroughbreds, and several others—but it all began in England. There is no special color for the breed, the range is vast. One of the original animals used to establish the breed was a stallion known as the Alcock Arab. He showed up in England during the reign of Queen Anne, between 1702 and 1714. He was a gray, and some people say that his influence was so strong that all gray Thoroughbreds today trace to him. Others say another horse, another gray, the Brownlow Turk, was responsible in part. But Thoroughbreds today can also be any of the chestnuts and browns, with all kinds of markings. This is a handsome, elegant horse with a refined head and big, intelligent eyes. The average height is 16.1 hands (sixty-five inches), although there is quite a spread in size.

The Thoroughbred line, once it was established, was assured of immortality by its incorporation into other breeds. No one can say for certain how many other breeds owe part of their quality to the Thoroughbred, but we know they include the American Saddle horse or Kentucky Saddler, the Tennessee Walking horse, the Morgan, the American and English Hackney horse, the Cleveland Bay, Irish Cob, Irish Hunter, Polish Poznan, the German Oldenburg, and the Hungarian Furioso horse. There are undoubtedly many others. In and of itself, and in the lines of many other magnificent breeds, the Thoroughbred is here to stay.

You can buy your child a very nice little Thoroughbred for about $1,000, or you can buy a proven champion stud who has made it at Madison Square Garden and spend a quarter of a million dollars. That's one of the nice things about the Thoroughbred, there's one for almost every pocketbook! It is unlikely that the Thoroughbred will ever relinquish its number-one position in the world of sport and recreation. People may breed better Thoroughbreds, but they are unlikely to come up with a better breed. The Thoroughbred is and probably always will be the royalty of horsedom. Look at one sometime, really look, and you will know why.

Standardbred Horse: In 1849 a stallion was born whose name was Hambletonian 10. He was destined to be the father of 1,321 foals and to be the foundation sire of the pacers and trotters we now see on the trotting tracks in America. We call the breed the Standardbred.

The American Standardbred is slightly smaller than the trotters and pacers of England, running from fourteen to sixteen hands, with weights from nine hundred to thirteen hundred pounds. Almost all Standardbreds are shown in harness. A few are so finely put together that they can go under saddle, but they really aren't made for that kind of competition against Saddlebreds and Hackneys, and certainly not against Thoroughbreds. But when it comes to endurance, energy, and quick, intelligent response to the driver's wishes, the Standardbred is the horse that is called for.

When we speak of animals of the historical significance of Hambletonian 10, the records are good, and we can sometimes go further back in time. Hambletonian was clearly the foundation animal for today's trotters and pacers, but he had a grandsire, an English

Thoroughbred called Messenger, that can be credited with being the true base for today's harness-racing horses.

Today's trotters and pacers show a great variety of color: bay, black, brown, chestnut, dun, gray, roan, sorrel, and even multicolor. They have a certain gameness that sets them apart, with what horse people speak of as overall quality. That means they look good, act good, have power and staying qualities. Many trotters are bred in Kentucky, but there are farms all over the country. Closely related to the Standardbred are the Hackney horse, the Morgan, and the Tennessee Walker. Selective breeding, training, and the weighted shoes used all combine to give the trotter its distinctive high-stepping gait. The energy it employs in a single race is almost beyond belief.

Morgan Horse: Recently, I was traveling in the Badlands of North Dakota with some friends. Near the beautiful little town of Medora we came up over a ridge, and spread out below was a small herd of Morgans, a string of saddle horses owned and maintained in the area. A Bay stallion stood on a prominence, his mane blowing in the wind, while his herd of thirty-five mares and foals moved about in the canyon below. Looking down on that incredibly beautiful scene, I couldn't help but reflect on the remarkable horse that started it all.

A man named Justin Morgan was born in West Springfield, Massachusetts, in 1747, the descendant of English settlers. Although sick with tuberculosis, he managed a career as a schoolteacher and a singer, but he was never physically strong. Through means or under circumstances that are not clear to us, he came into possession of a colt that had been born in 1790, and he named that horse after himself, Justin Morgan. The ancestry of the horse Justin Morgan is not clear, but there was certainly Arab in him, probably Turk, and possibly some Barb. It is even claimed there was heavy workhorse in his background. Justin Morgan was not a large horse—by the standards we recognize today he was a pony, standing fourteen hands at the withers, or fifty-six inches. By some chance, he was put to stud instead of being gelded, and thereby arises our tale.

The young stallion had a delicate, well-modeled head, a tapering neck, short legs, a short back testifying to his Arab blood, and extremely heavy shoulders with great width in the brisket. He was mild and even-tempered, although powerful and active. This horse, one of the most remarkable of all time, reproduced himself perfectly time and time again in conformation and in manners. In the words of the breeder, he was stunningly prepotent. He died at the age of thirty-one, in 1821, but by that time he had created a new breed of horse, one named after him, the Morgan. Even to-day, 186 years after this remarkable, powerful little animal was foaled, his prepotency is in evidence. Morgan colts today carry, as clearly as Justin Morgan's own first-generation colts, the stamp of this stallion. The superb bloodline descended from that first Morgan horse has helped develop the Tennessee Walking horse, the American Albino, the American Saddlebred, and the Standardbred horse. Through three main lines, his blood came down through time, through his colts Sherman, Bulrush, and Woodbury; any good Morgan can be traced back to those three sons and through them to their father.

Today Morgans are used under saddle, for showing, racing at a trot, jumping, and stock handling, testifying to their intelligence and versatility. They are used in harness, in shows, as singles and doubles, and in pulling contests, for they are immensely powerful for their size. They are also used for general utility and farm work—in fact, wherever and whenever a quality horse is required.

That was the gift of Justin Morgan, the horse and the man. There is no such thing as a pureblood Morgan because you cannot produce pureblood animals from a single parent, but still the horse and the breed live on in generation after generation because of the incredible power of this single pony-sized stallion, surely one of the most remarkable animals that ever lived.

Pinto: What do these words mean to you: *Pintado, Overo, Tobiano?* To me, they spell a western legend.

The Pinto has been recognized as a breed since 1963, but its history dates back to animals brought here by the Spaniards. The name Pinto comes from the Spanish *pintado*, which means "painted" or "spotted." There were once four kinds of Pintos in the Americas: the Overo, the Tobiano, the Appaloosa, and the Morocco spotted horse. The Appaloosa is no longer considered a paint. It is a breed apart. The Overo is the most common form in South America, although examples are found up here as well. In the Overo, the colors are primary—black, bay, brown, dun, roan, or sorrel. White is the secondary color, and one leg is always white, although sometimes only on a boot. The belly is white, and the back is colored. The head is either part or all white.

In the Tobiano, the primary color is white, with black, brown, dun, or sorrel secondary. The legs are white, and the head is either dark or, at least, marked with a dark color. The Morocco is white with ten percent or less dark markings.

Pintos come in three basic types. There is the parade

type, usually of American Saddlebred, Arab, and Thoroughbred lineage; there is the stock type, down from Arabs, Morgans, and Quarter horses; and there is the pleasure type, which can be of any breeding origin. They run from fourteen to sixteen hands. They are very flashy and have earned a following on that count alone. They can jump, and they are fine under English saddle as well as western.

Because they are so startling, American Pintos suffer from a prejudice. People find it difficult to think of them as anything but western horses under heavy Spanish leather and silver. Not so! Pintos are responsive animals and are especially good with children. They are steady, strong, and move well. If you are lucky enough to own a really startling example of the breed, you will attract more attention at a show than you would in a Rolls-Royce at a sports-car rally. Eastern show riders sometimes look on western-style horses as a notch below their own favorite types. The Pinto is one horse that can put that kind of nonsense to bed for good.

Cage Birds: If you have limited room and limited time to care for a pet, that doesn't rule you out. You can add color and movement and sound to your life by owning a cage bird or two.

The hobby is known as aviculture, the cultivation of birds, and it is widespread. From the canary owner to the breeder of exotic swans and pheasants, millions of people enrich their own lives with bird life. The field is such a large one, the differences between, say, breeding swans and geese and keeping a finch are so vast, generalizations are a little hard to come by. But here are some basic thoughts.

Birds are active, warm-blooded animals with a high rate of metabolism, and I cannot believe any bird likes being put into a cage so small he can't really get in a good glide and flap every now and then, and then being kept in that cage alone for all the days of his life. Birds need room. They have wings to spread and a curiosity to satisfy.

Think in terms of an aviary built into your home or apartment rather than a wee little cage on a bean pole of a stand. You can build an aviary out of scrap, plus a few things bought at your hardware store, for next to nothing, all for less than a fancy prison of a cage would cost you. Make certain your bird pet is properly placed vis-à-vis windows and drafts and direct sunlight. Your bird should be able to adjust himself to some degree.

Another thing: keep them clean. A dirty cage or aviary will invite ectoparasites, will cause your birds to develop unnatural habits, and can cause diseases of the foot. Remember, the bird can't do anything for himself in captivity, so you must do everything for him.

Birds don't like drafts, and they don't like cold rooms. On the other hand, they aren't very happy about being baked alive, either. They shouldn't be left in bright sunlight without shade available, should they feel they want it. Here again, the bird is your captive and can't get up and move its own cage.

If you anticipate keeping a bird as a pet, you should make it a point to find out what a complete diet consists of. Check with a zoo, an ornithologist, some good reference books, anyone and anything you feel you can really trust to tell you the whole truth, or at least admit they don't know it. Diets may be simple, one or two kinds of seed, or may be complicated, depending, of course, on the species of the birds involved. Some birds should have animal fat such as suet added to their diet, others require special types of seeds and certain oils added to their dry food. Some birds need fresh fruit on a pretty steady basis. It seems to me it is the determination of these facts that should come first.

Personally, I'm against keeping any animal without company. I can't see keeping one of anything caged for a lifetime. Get two (which means you have to pick a species of which you can get two). Give the pet you say you love an opportunity to be happy. Then, if he doesn't want to be happy, that's his problem. But at least give him a chance.

Some birds are restricted and are illegal to keep, at least without a permit. Check into these matters before ordering a bird through a pet shop or mail-order supplier. Don't get large birds unless you can supply very large cages, and make sure species are compatible before mixing them in a community cage. Don't buy a bird whose diet is going to be too expensive or too complicated for you to handle. Being a human being isn't all that difficult, all you have to do is think about the other guy, even if he is a birdbrain.

Bird Feeders: There are still things you can do in this world that cost only pennies and that can bring enormous pleasure into your life, just simple, private things like helping the birds where you live survive the winter to sing again next spring. Any man, woman, or child can prepare and maintain a bird feeder throughout the worst of the winter months. The results of their efforts undoubtedly will be life for smaller creatures, life that would otherwise hang on the thinnest of threads.

There are scores of books and pamphlets on bird feeders, so I won't give carpentry lessons here, except to say that even if you don't want to drive a single nail or buy a bird feeder from a garden-supply store, you can still put out a couple of foil pie plates and keep them stocked with commercial wild-bird seed. The birdseed you will need is as close as the pet-food department of your local supermarket or hardware store or pet shop. Buy the big bags, by the way, preferably the twenty-five-pounders. It's a lot cheaper, and you will be less likely to run out on the day of the blizzard.

Even people who regularly feed wild birds can overlook the critical matter of water. Birds need water every day of their lives, and they can't get it from eating snow or breaking through ice. So wild birds often must hunt over many square miles in their search for a little open water to keep them alive. Put out big plastic bowls of lukewarm water every day, and if they freeze, bring them in and refill them. There are electric anti-freezing devices available if you want one.

The commercially prepared birdseeds I mentioned are a basic food. You can add bread and pastry scraps or a small quantity of fruit. Even cheese has its fans. Suet, animal fat obtained for pennies at your butcher shop, is marvelous when rolled into balls and hung from trees in loose netting or packed into small cups that can be firmly anchored in place. Roll a few nuts in the suet or some peanut butter, and add in bacon fat from the morning feast. Leftover dry cereal, crumbs from the bottom of the cracker box, all can help preserve delicate little lives.

Bird feeders, for the amateur craftsmen, can be an interesting challenge. I have seen dozens of attractive branch-sitters and ground designs. All are variations on the themes of kindness and compassion and the humanity that our race has been claiming for so long. If your children are old enough, put them in charge of keeping the feeders stocked and of spreading some bird food out away from the house for birds too shy to approach. The kind of lessons a child can learn from this kind of responsibility can only be good.

A word of caution, if you have cats and dogs with a taste for fresh songbirds: place your feeders high, and don't spread food on the ground. That wouldn't be fair.

The Aquarium: The people in the home-aquarium industry tell me that there are four to five million serious aquarists in America today, people who maintain aquariums of various sizes and degrees of complexity. The big question is, of course, how do you start? In a word, slowly. The ideal starting unit, I think, is ten to twenty gallons. You can start with five, of course, or twenty-five, but in my opinion, ten to twenty gallons is the perfect starting range. This isn't so overwhelming that you can't get used to things before taking the big plunge, and it isn't so small that you can't make a really lovely addition to your home short of selling the family car. You should start with a full kit, though, with pump and filtration system, with lights and thermostatic controls, but none of that is as expensive as you may think. There are really first-rate books on the subject, so dig into them before you add the living creatures.

One question often asked is, "Should I start with a marine aquarium or a freshwater unit?" The answer is the latter. The marine or saltwater aquarium is for the expert. The fish generally cost many times as much, and nothing is more discouraging for the beginner than to find a thirty-five-dollar reef fish floating belly up in the tank. What about real plants versus plastic plants? Open to several opinions, but mine is that real plants are an art in themselves, and the average aquarist is very poor at it. For the beginner, the plastic plants look exactly the same and offer no problems. Start with plastic, learn to keep fish alive, and then, if you are so inclined, learn to keep plants alive. Nothing says you can't mix the two, by the way. Now, what kind of fish do you start with? Very inexpensive ones. The dealer who tries to hustle the novice into expensive fish is not playing square. You are going to lose fish in the early stages, until both you and your tank are functioning. Spend a couple of months with old-fashioned Guppies, some Mollies perhaps, and a few other inexpensive species. There will be time enough to go for the real exotics.

Fish for the New Aquarium: Once you have set up a new aquarium in your home, what fish should you start with? Before "which," though, comes the question "how many?" You don't want to overpopulate your tank, for that leads to a shortage of oxygen, to stress, disease, and a lot of dead fish. A good basic rule is *one inch of fish for each half-gallon of water.* If you have a twenty-gallon tank, you shou'' plan on eventually having forty inches of fish. You can break that down any way you want to: twenty one-inch fish plus forty one-half-inch fish, or ten two-inch fish plus five four-inch fish. The combinations are endless. You don't have to climb into the tank with a tape measure and start measuring fish, but the general rule can guide you.

As for kinds of fish, there are hundreds to choose from. Some are more readily available in one area than another, some in one season than another. You have to find the good pet or aquarium stores near you and shop. If you want a community tank, you are again dealing with almost limitless combinations. Guppies are always a favorite. They are quite splendid, small, and hardy. They get along with almost anything except those species that eat them. The Barbs, Swordtails, Platys, Mollies, Angelfish, Zebra Danios, Neon Tetras all make lovely fish as long as there is some compatibility of size. Large fish eat small fish, so don't put a whale of a tropical in with your Guppies and your Neon Tetras, or one day you will find yourself with one very large fish.

Any knowledgeable pet-shop owner can guide you. He will warn you to beware of Gouramis, for instance, because they can be bullies. He will tell you to leave the Oscars and Jack Dempseys alone if you have a community tank, and he will tell you which catfish are a good buy. Most but not all catfish make out just fine in a community tank.

Start with inexpensive fish, and slowly build your tank's population until it approximates that half-gallon-to-the-inch rule. In time, you will know more about it than anyone else around.

Small Rodent Pets: When space is a problem, or when the landlord says no to cats and dogs, small rodents make satisfying, inexpensive pets.

Hamsters are small, virtually tailless, desert rodents from the Middle East. They come in a variety of coat and color styles, and are clean and just about odorless. Very interesting, inexpensive hamster-ariums are manufactured and sold everywhere pets are found. You can create your own hamster utopia with play and sleep areas and endless tunnels.

Gerbils are also desert rodents. In the wild, the fifty-four different kinds range through Africa, the Middle East, and many parts of arid Asia. They have nice long tails and are gentle little animals that can live as long as five years. They, too, enjoy elaborate housing and tunnel complexes.

Guinea pigs are not pigs and do not come from Guinea, which is in Africa, but from Peru. They are rodents, of course, and again come in a variety of colors and coats. They are very precocious and breed when very young, giving birth to babies that are on their feet and away minutes after birth. Guinea pigs are larger than hamsters and gerbils, much larger, and need a pen rather than an enclosed cage. They are not the escape artists the others are.

Prepared foods are available in the pet department of your supermarket or your pet shop for all three animals. The pet shop has the added advantage of having new cage ideas. All three animals should be protected from cats and dogs in the house, and all three should have food and water all the time. Water is supplied in a bottle and not an open dish.

These small rodents are not difficult or expensive to obtain; they are not time-consuming or expensive to maintain. The only real problem is that they reproduce at a staggering rate, and people almost inevitably get the sexes confused. Just recently, my daughter's male guinea pig, Trouble by name, gave birth to twins. We owned as how we had made a mistake about *his* gender and that he was a she who had become involved with her brother. But then her brother gave birth, and we still haven't got that one sorted out. Keep your sexes separated, if you can figure out who's who and what's up.

Mice and Rats as Pets: Over two million mice are sold in pet shops every year, and a good number of rats as well. Do they make good pets? Yes, they do. For the shut-in, the person with very limited means or space, or the person who cannot have a larger pet for any of a variety of reasons, mice and rats are near perfect. They are active and fun, and they seldom bite if handled regularly and carefully. They are easy to

from their rays can cause anything from pain to death. Advanced aquarists are against the idea of outlawing venomous fish, and perhaps they are right. People contemplating their purchase, however, should be sure they know what they are doing and be sure that no one else is going to stick his hand in the tank. Seek out an ichthyologist at the nearest museum, college, or aquarium, and talk it over with him. These fish will not kill you in seconds or any other such nonsense, but they will make you sick. They can, in some instances, kill. My advice is simple. Make sure you know what you are doing. Do a lot of reading, and ask a lot of questions first. Get the fish only after all that is behind you. As for venomous snakes, they should *only* be kept by experts. The element of risk is always there, and only those with the experience and maturity to evaluate that risk should be allowed to take it.

Keeping Exotic Pets: Americans now have over 123 breeds of dogs to select from, unlimited variations among the random-bred dogs, and all kinds of cats, tropical fish, and standard cage birds, but for some people, this still isn't enough. There are all kinds of reasons, I suppose, why some people have wild animals in their homes. Perhaps they need to be different, or to flirt with disaster, or to state through their pets something of their own personality that they are unable to express themselves.

Not long ago, a large American city held a closed-bid mail auction for what it termed "surplus zoo animals." Before it was too late, after the bids were opened but before any animals were shipped, the parks commissioner ordered all animals held until the buyers could be checked out. Each one was interviewed when he or she was not already known to the investigator. One man had bid high on two jaguars and a grown bobcat. When interviewed, he said he planned to put a cage in the backyard. He did not know how big jaguars grew to be, assuming it was under a hundred pounds (they can actually approach three hundred in captivity, where obesity is the rule). He did not know they can leap thirty-five feet, or how much they ate. In short, a man without any experience, knowledge, or skill was about to buy, in blissful ignorance, three cats, at least two of which were likely to kill him someday. Few jaguars remain tractable through maturity, and even if they are successfully socialized, they are still animals with hair-triggers and unsocializable reflexes.

Less than a year before this auction took place, a fifteen-year-old boy in Philadelphia bought a cobra from a catalog. It was shipped, no questions asked, and the boy was bitten. He nearly died. When will this traffic in wild and exotic animals stop? Zoos are where they belong, when they are not in the wild, and it is entirely predictable that injuries are going to continue to occur and animals are going to be removed from natural habitats and shipped under appalling conditions until the sale of these animals to unqualified private citizens is halted. There are private parties with great expertise working on valid propagation projects, and their owning some of these animals can be justified. But surely the person who should own a cobra or jaguar is the exceptional person and should be required to demonstrate that clearly enough to be licensed for the privilege.

None of the wild cats belong cooped up as pets, that is categorical. The question always asked is Can the big, wild cats be tamed? Yes, they can, but their reflexes can't. The most gentle of big cats, and small wild cats, too, can be set off by the most innocuous-seeming situation. With a big cat, that can quickly spell disaster, and has on more than a few occasions.

Now that wolves are getting rare in most areas except Alaska and Canada, many people want to keep wolves in their homes. The man who buys himself a wolf cub is in for a few surprises. You cannot punish a wolf, he will not take it from you; which means you are very unlikely ever to housebreak a wolf. Wolves terrify people, neighbors complain, and your lawyer ends up trying to convince the courts that you really aren't breaking the law when, in fact, you really are. Wolves are among my very favorite animals, and I have handled them more than once, but I can tell a future wolf owner he had better learn wolf language. A wolf is a lover one minute and a wolf the next.

I've known some exotic-pet owners who were silly, some who were cruel, and I've known more than a few who were nuts, but most were just plain misguided. Before you buy a wild animal to take into your home, talk it over with an expert. Go by the zoo, and see the appropriate curator, and listen to what he has to say. He will have been asked the same questions dozens of times before. Listen to him very carefully. The chances are you will change your mind.

Monkeys as Pets: Monkeys are the exotic creatures most frequently selected by pet owners who want to be different, and monkeys make *terrible* pets. Once a monkey reaches sexual maturity, the chances that it will not bite are slim, and a monkey bite can be a messy affair. It is as bad as the bite of a pig or of a man. Monkeys are virtually impossible to toilet train, and bringing one into the family is exactly like having an infant who will never grow up. Monkeys smell! They will use their food and water dishes for a toilet and will often play with their own wastes and throw the stuff around the room. They probably don't do this in the wild, but as a reaction to captivity.

Very few veterinarians know much about monkeys, and if yours gets sick, you are in for some possibly expensive trouble. Through a process called zoonosis, man and monkey can exchange a number of diseases up to and including tuberculosis. If you get a cold, you are likely to give your baby monkey pneumonia. A number of monkey handlers in Germany died recently of a brain virus that they picked up from their charges.

Apes are worse problems yet. A full-grown chimp can kill a man, and many have been known to try. Gibbons are collected by shooting the mothers out of trees and collecting the babies that haven't been killed in the fall. Most of them will die before making it into a home anyway. How's that for animal-loving!

Don't you believe the pet-shop owner who tells you a monkey eats some rabbit pellets, a slice of bread, and a wedge of apple. That's not a monkey diet, it's a short cut to malnutrition and death! Monkeys have complicated diets. Some species should be fed as many as twenty-three different foods *every* day! They require bone meal, egg, meat—yes, meat—vitamins, tropical fruits, even in the winter when they're expensive. And don't look to the zoo to take your pet off your hands when you become fed up, bitten, or broke. Most zoos won't touch any kind of pet, much less a monkey.

Putting a monkey in a cage is cruel. Subjecting it to strange noises and air pollution while denying it the opportunity to respond reflexively by seeking altitude is torture. So is denying it a chance to mate and to live in a structured monkey society, for monkeys are sexy, sociable creatures. Don't you be the villain. Let wild animals stay wild, the way they were intended to be.

There are plenty of dogs and cats to choose from, animals genetically engineered by man for man.

The Strangest Pet of All: All kinds of people have kept all kinds of pets, but now I have met the strangest pet of all, an aardvark. On a recent trip to Africa, we visited with filmmaker-naturalist Alan Root at his home on the shores of Lake Naivasha in central Kenya. Alan has a pet aardvark. I don't know anyone else about whom one can make that statement.

Alan has named his aardvark Million. Can you guess why? Think of the song . . . "Aardvark a million miles for one of your smiles" (don't blame me, blame Alan Root).

Million belongs to a strange offshoot of the animal kingdom known as the Tubilidentata. It is all alone out there on its biological limb because it really doesn't have any relatives very close in. Also called the earth pig, the aardvark burrows into the earth like a hot knife cutting butter. Those long claws on those powerful front legs go like fury. Million is very friendly with almost everyone, but she especially likes Alan, who has allowed her to make a positive mess of the yard. When she sees Alan, this one-hundred-pound-plus bundle of bristly, porky charm gets all kittenish. She charges Alan, then just before impact, rolls a perfect somersault at his feet, often between his feet, and is gone. Actually, that is a natural thing for an aardvark to do. If grabbed from above before it can burrow underground, an aardvark does a somersault to either break the neck of the animal grasping it or rips its belly open with its long digging claws. But with Alan and approved guests, Million's intentions are pure love and play.

In the normal context of American life, I am opposed

to most exotic pets, almost all, really, but things are a little different in East Africa, and Alan Root is a naturalist, so I guess this is the exception that makes the rule right, or something like that. Anyway, you may never have considered an aardvark for a pet, and you can't get one if you want one, but I thought you would want to know about Million. Can you believe that? Aardvark a million miles!

The Baboon and the Baby: One of the saddest tales I ever heard about a pet is a true story handed down to us by a super but almost unknown South African nature writer, Eugene Maiais. He tells it in his book *My Friends the Baboons*.

Years ago, on a farm called Stypsteenkop, between the towns of Warmaths and Rooiberg, there was a pet baboon. It was quite a character and something of a family treasure. When the young mistress of the farm gave birth to a child, the baboon took enormous interest in the infant although, of course, it wasn't allowed near it. Whenever the monkey saw the baby, it made the cooing affectionate sounds these animals usually reserve for their own young. Then, one tragic day, the baboon broke its chains, and the mother and a maid heard the infant crying. They rushed into the bedroom and saw the baboon sitting on the windowsill holding the baby. It bared its teeth to warn them away. Before anything could be done, the baboon made for a very high tree that overhung the house. The more they tried to coax it down, the higher it climbed, taking the infant with it. At some points, it would hold the infant by an ankle and dangle it, then it would hug it again.

The mother standing below was, of course, in an absolute panic. Her husband was away, and she was afraid the baboon would get bored with its new game and simply drop the baby. That would have meant certain death. Then the maid remembered a bushman who had once worked on the farm and had been a friend to the baboon when it was young. She ran off and in time—it must have been an eternity for the mother—she returned with the old man. He made everyone leave, go into the house, and shut all the doors and windows. He began talking to the baboon using a special language bushmen are said to use in dealing with animals. Slowly the baboon came down from the tree and moved up to the bushman. The old man fastened the chain to the monkey's collar and put his hands out. The baboon handed him the baby, a little scratched but essentially unharmed. I wonder what was in that baboon's eyes when it surrendered the child, and what was in the bushman's. The baboon was shot, of course, and the baby grew up. We don't know what happened to the bushman. He went back to his wild places. One small story out of millions about man and animal and what they do to and for each other.

Yacky the Duck: This is the story of an orphan. We don't know about the early days of Yacky's life, only that one morning a very small and very fluffy brown-and-yellow duckling showed up on a neighbor's doorstep. In haste, the apparently orphaned youngster was delivered to us—to my daughter, especially, for she has a super record with infant animals. The baby peeped incessantly, and the name Yacky was attached. And then Yacky grew, oh my did she grow! I thought she would end up the world's first duckbilled, web-footed ostrich. She got to be mallard size, then once and a half mallard size, then about twice mallard size. She is a Roven, a domestic strain of mallard.

Pamela taught Yacky to swim—it was summer by now—but Yacky wouldn't stay in the water two minutes without Pamela inches away. She would wail and carry on the minute her new mother was out of sight, and when she was tired, she would climb on top of my daughter's head and ride around in the water that way. Yacky was eventually placed on a nearby farm and was banded so that she wouldn't be eaten by mistake. She found a handsome young drake to her liking, and then the eggs appeared. Prudence, her daughter, was hatched (the spitting image of Yacky), and then old Yack turned up with a son, William. We think she stole him since he is obviously half Peking, a handsome devil.

For a number of reasons, Yacky and her children Prudence and William have returned to our yard where they now live quite happily, if noisily. Neither Yacky nor Prudence ever shuts up. Every now and then, Yacky is allowed in the house where she does her favorite thing: she assaults cats and dogs. Striding from room to room, she sends cats and English Bulldogs and Golden Retrievers and Siberian Huskies flying in all directions. Reckoning the best defense is an offense, Yacky is as offensive as she can be with other animals. You have never seen a really scandalous look until you have seen a Siamese cat all curled up in the sun suddenly zapped in the you-know-what by a rude duck. No one gets hurt, almost everyone gets insulted, and Yacky the nut has the time of her life. She doesn't stop until she nails everyone. Fortunately, she is too fat to follow her victims under sofas, chairs, and beds, and once the coast is cleared, once everyone has been forced to acknowledge that Yacky is queen of all she beholds, Yacky does something very unpleasant on the floor and is hastened out of doors. Anyway, Yacky is one more reason the Caras clan enjoys life and living. It's much more fun than being normal.

INDEX